Hamlyn all-colour paperbacks

Eileen King
Toys and Dolls for Collectors

Hamlyn · London

FOREWORD

Toys were for many years the poor cousins of the antiques' world. The fact that they have become increasingly collected, and sufficiently respectable to have sales devoted to them in the leading auction rooms, is an indication of their changed status. In compiling this short guide for collectors both the publisher and I felt that, wherever possible, we should avoid illustrations of toys that have already been used in other books and thus make the illustrations meaningful both to established and new collectors.

Many of the toys come from the collection which my husband and I have formed over eight years. Restoration has been carried out on some toys that were literally falling apart when purchased, and some of the dolls bought without clothes have been redressed in fabrics of their period.

I should like to express my thanks to the Worthing, Colchester, Bethnal Green, London, The Guild Hall, British and Rottingdean Museums and Platt Hall, Manchester, who allowed the photographing of exhibits, and also to Mrs H. Sebastian, Lt Peter Edwards R.N., Miss Gaby Goldscheider, Mrs K. Brott, Mrs J. Marsh, Miss Georgina Pritchard and Mrs K. Reddick.

The inclusion of objects ranging in value from a few pence to several hundred pounds should give some indication of the variety of collectable toys that are available on the market.

E.K.

(Title-page illustration) The Crandall Great Show Acrobats.

Published by the Hamlyn Publishing Group Limited
London · New York · Sydney · Toronto
Astronaut House, Feltham, Middlesex, England

Copyright © The Hamlyn Publishing Group Limited 1973

ISBN 0 600 38679 1
Phototypeset by Filmtype Services Limited, Scarborough
Printed by Sir Joseph Causton & Sons Ltd.,
London and Eastleigh

CONTENTS

- 4 **The History of Toys**
- 20 **The Nineteenth Century**
  Paper Dolls. Children's Books.
  Educational Toys. Money-Boxes.
  Tin Toys. Trains. Soldiers.
  Theatres. Optical Toys. Farms
  and Noah's Arks. Horses and Carts.
  Wheeled Toys. Board Games. Shops.
  Miniature Furniture. Toy China.
  Dolls' House Furniture and Dolls'
  Houses. Cots, Beds and Cradles.
  Acrobatic Toys. Musical Toys and
  Automata.
- 92 **Dolls**
  Wax. Wooden. Porcelain. Papier-
  Mâché and Composition. Parian.
  Bisque. French. German. Pedlars.
  Rubber. Tin. Celluloid. Character.
- 138 **The Twentieth Century**
  Teddy Bears
- 142 **Places to Visit**
- 144 **Dolls' Marks**
- 152 **Repairing and Fakes**
- 153 **Glossary**
- 156 **Books to Read**
- 157 **Index**

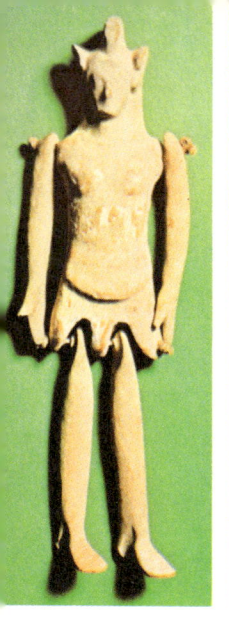

Basic toys. A jointed doll made of clay, fifth century BC, from Athens, and a pull-along terracotta horse, Roman, fourth century AD

THE HISTORY OF TOYS
Early Times

In considering the playthings of early man, scant evidence survives. Small doll-like figures are known, but their preservation and the presence of some recognized fertility symbols suggest a votive, rather than play object. Life being a question of survival, there would have been little time to carve a toy for a child, though a baby might have a rattle fashioned to amuse him. When communities become established, figures and models are found, so that in the remains of early civilization are discovered all the basic toys, such as balls, hoops, skittles and dolls.

Small moveable models, such as an Egyptian bronze tiger, which can open and close its mouth, survive, and there are several examples of early pull-along horses. Though Greek children were given toys, such as knucklebones, hobby horses and boats, they were expected to surrender them at a temple when very young. It is known that children of the period built model houses, but did they really furnish them with fine bronze furniture, as is sometimes suggested? Small votive figures of lead, which look like the flat-back soldiers of the eighteenth century, were found in the sanctuary of Artemis Orthia, but had they been found elsewhere they too might now be classified as toys.

Childhood was of extremely short duration in the Dark Ages, but the lack of surviving toys should not lead us to suppose that mothers suddenly cried: 'No more playing with toys. The Dark Ages are upon us!' Obviously children played with basic toys as they had over the centuries.

Surviving medieval pottery toys come mainly from Germany, which had an embryonic toy-making industry by the Middle Ages. There are also contemporary surviving examples of miniature kitchen equipment, dolls of wood and china and engravings of animated fighting knights worked by strings.

Two miniature pots which were probably toys. A pewter ewer, fourteenth century, and a bronze cooking vessel, fourteenth to fifteenth century

A horn book from the London Museum, and *(right)* an American replica. The child learned his letters from such a board which was often carried tied to his belt

The Renaissance

The growth of the merchant classes in the fifteenth and sixteenth centuries led to the education of a greater number of children. A literate child could improve family business and, in a similar way, children of the aristocracy were valued mainly as pawns in the inheritance game, so that Sir Charles Verney could remark cheerfully on the death of a child, that he still had a baker's dozen, and Montaigne could write that two or three children were lost 'not without regret but without grief'.

The children's literature which was appearing taught the virtues of duty to parents and dedication in the pursuit of knowledge. Childhood appears to have been dreary, uncomfortable and to have ended quickly, yet prints of the day show a very different side to life. Children play with windmills, hobby horses, kites, cup-and-ball games, toy cradles, soldiers and dolls, and one sixteenth-century print of a street market shows a very wide assortment of dolls, drums, pikes, swords and horses.

Rich children were given the toys that really exhibit the splendour of the age. Among his possessions the Dauphin Louis XIII had his own small suit of armour, a silver cannon which he pulled along, a drum which was played by a female figure animated by string, and a peep-show worked by sand.

Craftsmen were now organising themselves into guilds, and restrictive practices existed even in the toy world, so that a doll's head could not be painted by the man who had turned

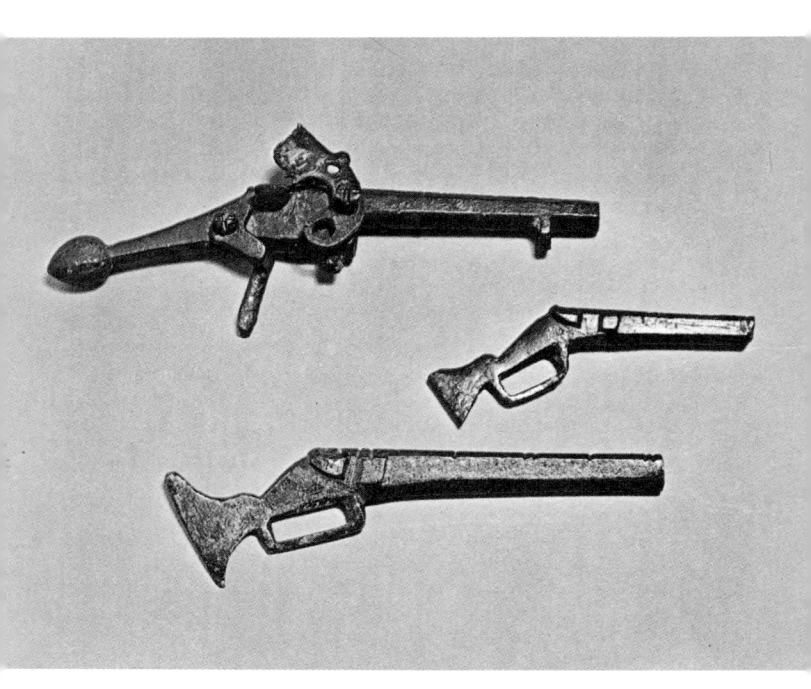

Model pistols made of metal, wheel lock and match lock, about 1600. The largest pistol is 4 ins. (10·2 cm.) long. Found in London

it. Most of the toys were made in Germany and the Netherlands, but some were obviously made in England, as the industry was protected by an import duty.

'Un Petit Ménage', a box containing all sorts of miniature objects of wood, pewter and china, which might delight a child, was a typical gift of the period. Many adults were amused by what appear to us as childish toys. The cup-and-ball game and pantins were played with avidly by adults, and royalty often exchanged gifts of model rooms and doll-like figures made in great detail. The cabinet rooms, which were furnished with fine silver models of everyday objects, were a feature of life for rich Dutch merchants, who used them as a means of displaying their wealth.

The drawing-room cabinets developed into the idea of a model house which could be furnished with objects of wood, china and pewter. Though many of the Nuremberg Baby Houses appear to be almost too perfect ever to have been played with by a child, some were certainly made for specific children, and rooms of furniture were often given as gifts. Some of these rooms were inhabited by finely dressed dolls of wax and wood, one doll-maker being said to make wax heads that were almost unbreakable.

The peasant child probably owned a few basic toys such as a drum, hoop or carved stump doll. At country fairs he might have been given gaily gilded gingerbread characters to be admired for a few hours and then eaten as he walked home, possibly carrying a windmill on a stick, as the modern child might do.

Very few toys of this period exist outside museums, though a stump doll was thrown on the fire recently as it had 'so little shape left, and woodworm'. Fake model soldiers of the period have been made and fairly modern primitive dolls sometimes parade under the title of stump dolls, so that scepticism rather than care should be exercised in buying any toys said to be made before the eighteenth century.

Dating from 1665, this engraving illustrates the wide variety of toys available in the seventeenth century. The cooking utensils on the bottom left are particularly interesting, as are the small musical instruments on which the musicians play

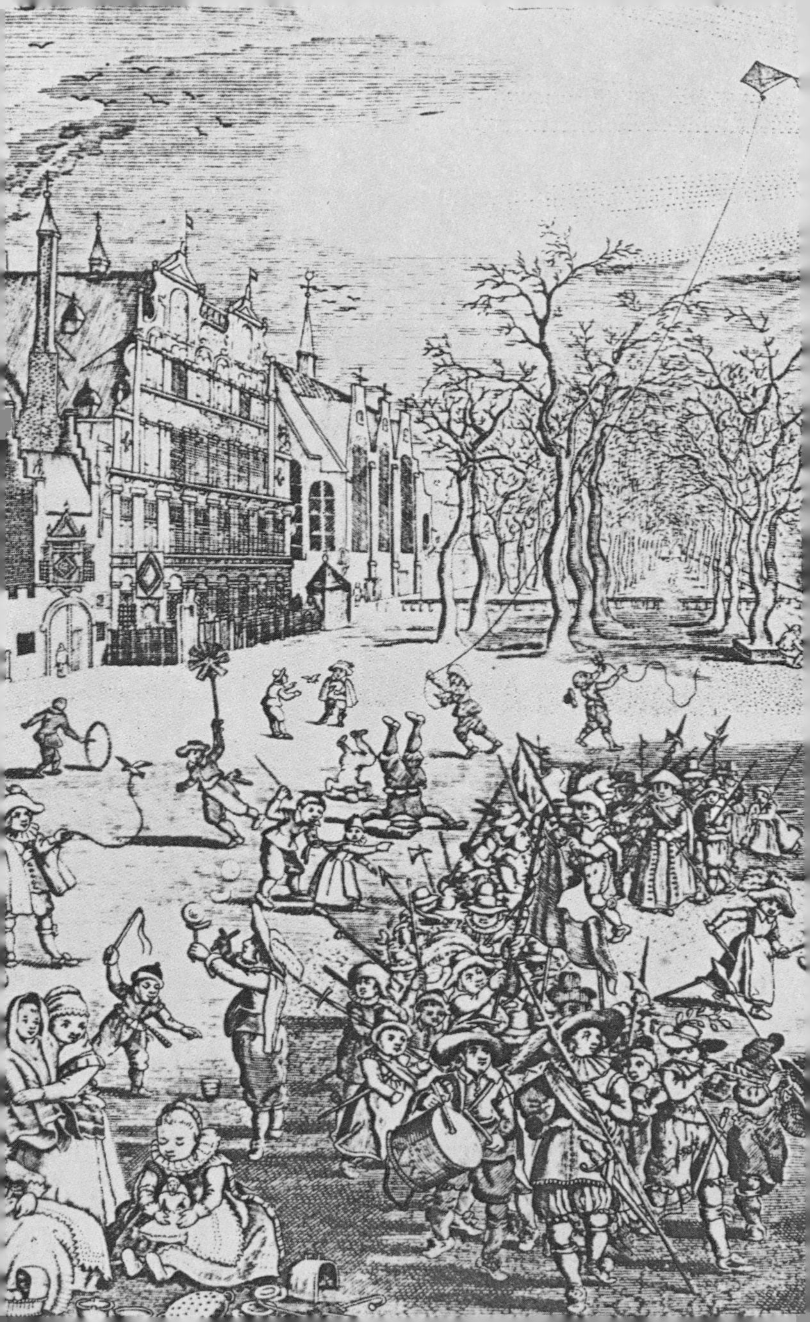

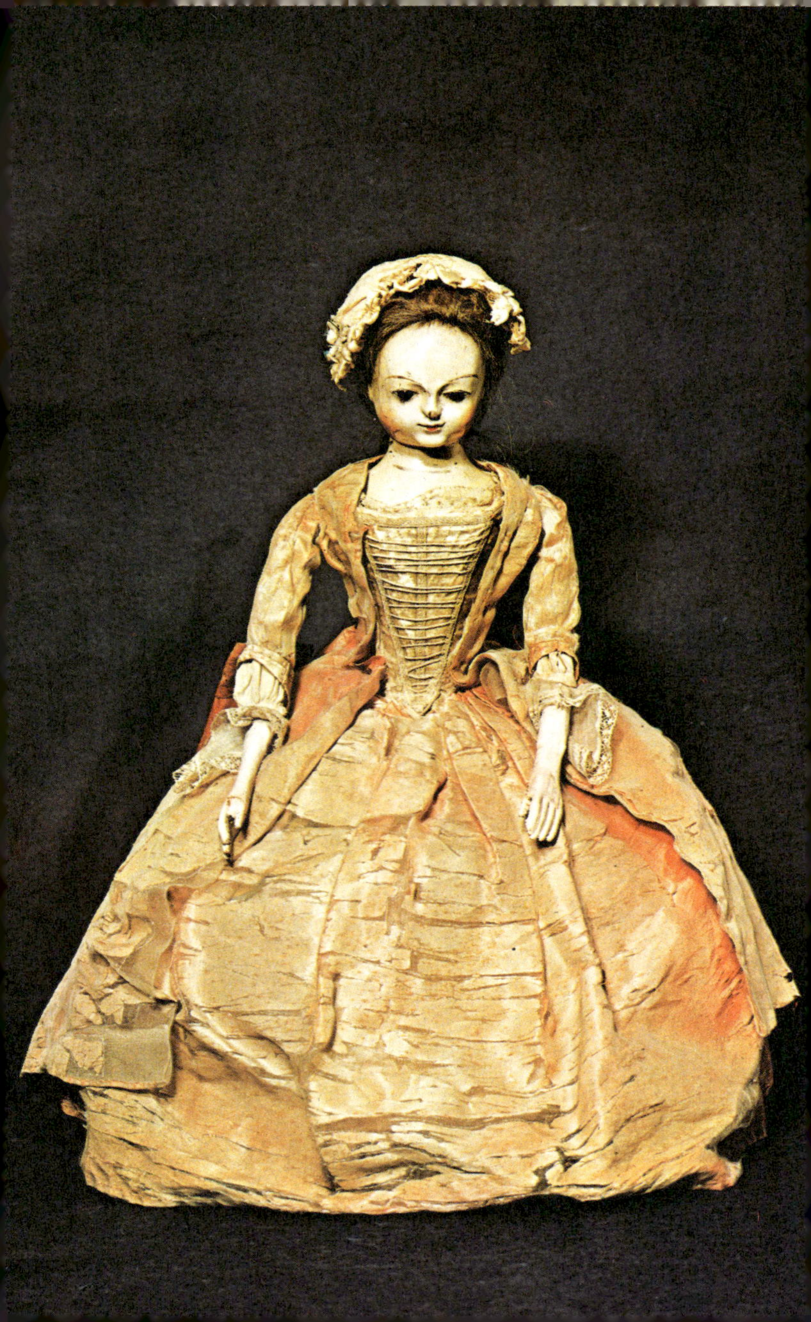

THE EIGHTEENTH CENTURY
Dolls

In considering dolls of this period, the collector thinks of those simply turned, wooden figures, with spade-like hands and black pupil-less eyes, known as Queen Anne dolls. As Anne died in 1714 and they continued to be made into the Regency period, the title should be taken lightly.

Germany, England and America, all produced dolls carved from one piece of wood. Rattle dolls of a similar type are found with gaily painted clothes. These toys typify those that were sold from pedlars' baskets and at fairs to the ordinary child.

Wax was becoming more attractive to the toymaker, and while some dolls have simple beads of wax forming their eyes, others had unusual mechanisms which made them cry and turn their heads. The insertion of hair into the scalp and glass eyes into the face became more common. Early wax heads were often mounted on wooden bodies, soon superseded by a stuffed cloth body.

Papier-Mâché dolls were made in Nuremberg and stuffed rag dolls were popular, though too fragile for survival.

Finely dressed wooden dolls were expensive but, as seen in prints and paintings, were played with. Mrs Delany, writing in 1776, talks of a doll for her godchild, which was bought undressed and sent to the hairdresser for a wig and the milliner for a hat, the lady herself making the numerous clothes for 'Miss Dolly Mode who would be so difficult to replace if broken'.

Wooden dolls, offered for sale, have often been mended and redressed over the years, which detracts from their value. A wooden torso with padded cloth or leather arms should not be ignored, as this was a method of manufacture. Though black enamelled eyes are the most common, some were painted and others made of blown glass and set into the gessoed and painted head.

A very fully dressed wooden Queen Anne doll, made between 1740 and 1760, wearing a flannel petticoat and blue knitted stockings under the silk dress. From the Gallery of English Costume, Platt Hall, Manchester

The Norwich House is a particularly well proportioned example of an eighteenth-century Baby House. Painted to represent brickwork

Dolls' Houses

The passion for assembling small, costly objects in a miniature house continued throughout the eighteenth century, so that we read of royal adults decorating *Baby Houses*, as they were known in England. Though the English houses were without the wealth of silver with which the Dutch packed their cabinets, they were nevertheless richly decorated, and furnished with fine and costly objects. There is a long tradition that architects and estate carpenters made dolls' houses as miniature versions of the Family House, but there appears to be very little evidence to substantiate this.

The highly desirable English and American Baby Houses have finely made façades, with elegantly proportioned windows and panelled doors. These houses were often mounted on a separate stand and were obviously intended as drawing-room exhibits rather than children's playthings, though often, sadly, finishing their days in the nursery.

In dating an old dolls' house, the weight and thickness of walls are a good guide. As they were made to carry a wealth of detail, the basic construction had to be solid. Quite often the weight necessitated carrying-handles on the sides, though this is not an obvious indication of great age, as I have in my collection several late Victorian houses which have these additions. A lock at the side of the house is of more reliability in dating, as it kept secure the valued contents.

No detail was too difficult for the eighteenth-century craftsman to imitate: balustrades, porticos and steps are all faithfully copied in miniature, as are metal grates, utensils and door furniture. Rooms often contain fine, built-in china display cabinets and well-proportioned fire-places and book-shelves. Houses of this period have a look of fine quality and make the mock Georgian dolls' houses made by modern enthusiasts look absurd.

The kitchen of the Norwich House boasts a very rare miniature spit, though the china is some hundred years later than the house

The Denton Welch Baby House dates from 1793 and stands on its original base with two useful drawers. Well finished interior

Shops which included furnishings for Baby Houses in their stock were known at the beginning of the eighteenth century, probably pandering to a craze for furnishing such houses, which had spread from the Low Countries. The possibility of there existing other, more cheaply-made houses for children, alongside the documented examples, is strong. Children had played with model rooms through the ages. Why should they have stopped in the early eighteenth century?

Finding contemporary furnishings for these old houses is extremely difficult, and so fine are the proportions that they look better left unfurnished than added to by fake copies, or even later Victorian furnishings which are easier to find. Many of the houses, which have been retained by the families who owned them, have had furniture added over the years, as would an actual family house, so that my view is probably a little over pure!

Miniature silver, china, glass, tin and pewter kitchenware had continued to be made over the centuries. Fine dressing mirrors, lowboys, chests of drawers, tables, pictures and beds were made in great detail and can be seen today in their original state in the Uppark Baby House, circa 1730, together with the dolls inhabiting it.

The eighteenth century is the age of golden names for the collector of dolls' houses; The Blackett House, Nostell Priory, and the attractive, but less grand Norwich House, all exercise tremendous appeal. The earliest American dolls' house is dated 1744 and is to be found in the Van Cortlandt Mansion in New York. As is so often the case with great grandeur, we come to the end of an era, for by the close of the century the houses have the look of a child's toy. The locks have been taken off and the proportions simplified to such an extent, that the dolls' house owned by Queen Victoria was virtually a box with a divider across the middle.

A typical example of an eighteenth-century Nuremberg kitchen with its interesting assortment of cooking utensils

A rather crudely modelled stage coach dating from 1790 and probably estate-made for a child. Interesting detail to wheels

Toys for Boys

Richard Edgeworth, the eighteenth-century pedagogue, and his daughter Maria, considered that as long as a child had the good sense to destroy his toys they could do him no great harm. Boys of the eighteenth century were obvious masters of this art as, in comparison with girls' toys, few survived. This is the age when toys were made for pure enjoyment. The jigsaw puzzle does not rear its lurking educational aims until the last years of the century. Toys, being cheaper, could now give pleasure to a much wider range of children.

Several attractive toy coaches are known but owe their survival mainly to the fact that they are often models to be admired, rather than toys. The Noah's Ark, a popular European toy since the sixteenth century, was often treated with care, one remaining complete with four hundred inhabitants! Roller skates, yo-yos, jack-in-the-boxes and bows and arrows all gave hours of enjoyment, together with games like Blow

Point, which directed arrows at numbers.

Lambs with gold-spangled fleece and metal legs and horns, made in a variety of sizes, were sold in the streets, together with gingerbread soldiers and simple books. Lead and tin soldiers were made in large numbers, especially by the firm of J. G. Hilpert of Nuremberg – the first firm to mark its products. Guns, trumpets, drums, and soldiers modelled on real warriors, helped in the battle-field simulation. Other soldiers were made of folded paper, a material which was increasingly used for children's toys.

This is the age of the sophisticated automata, many of which, being made of precious metals, could not have been ordinary playthings, though children had their own in base metals. Visual toys of all kinds were delighted in; peep-shows, sand pictures, and by the end of the century, model theatres, were given to the children, some up-to-date parents even giving boys miniature balloons to play with, in imitation of the current interest in ballooning.

A group of lead flat-backed soldiers on the march, made in Belgium about 1830

Made of carved and painted wood and decorated with a velvet seat, this toy moves on wheels neatly concealed under its feet

The Toy Horse

The hobby-horse is a toy that has continued to survive in various forms. Often illustrated in medieval and renaissance prints, they sometimes show the complete horse carved and attached to the end of a striped pole, though a simple head decorated with medallions, tinsel and ribbons was more common. A cross bar was sometimes added, and wheels gave a smoother ride along the ground. Though hobby-horses were made throughout the nineteenth century, they lost popularity, having been succeeded by the more satisfactory rocking-horse.

The earliest known horse on rockers dates from the seventeenth century, and is basically a rocking-boat shape, with a carved head at the front, and a back rest for the rider. One horse of the period has a pistol on its shoulder, while another has added realism with raised front legs. The boat-shaped sides were sometimes painted to form the legs of the horse, and from this developed the cutting away of the thick wood, to form free-standing legs. The familiar carved horse with outstretched legs on well balanced rockers, which was so typical of the eighteenth century, was thus evolved. These finely made models were sometimes covered with horse-skin, though genuine eighteenth-century examples tend by now to have assumed a rather macabre appearance, despite their fine harness, medallions and embossed saddles.

Horses on wheels had been popular since the sixteenth century. Turkish trumpeters and knights were among the characters depicted in bronze, wood and tin. The wheels were sometimes neatly concealed under the feet, but others stood on a wheeled wooden base. Some were large enough to carry one or two children, while others were a few inches high and made to be pulled along on a piece of ribbon or string.

A fine seventeenth-century wooden rocking-horse from the London Museum, with a dummy pistol set in a wooden holster conveniently placed for the young rider

THE NINETEENTH CENTURY

Childhood in the eighteenth century could have been a delight or horror, according to the beliefs of the sect or philosopher supported by the parent. The nineteenth century sees a far greater degree of conformity in methods of upbringing. Girls as well as boys were now often educated at school, and more effort was made by these establishments to discipline and teach, though often by cruel or bizarre methods.

Sunday Toys

The fast spread of the middle classes, and their desire to improve their children, led to the production of vast quantities of toys with an educational aim. Learning was usually based on religious teaching, and in church-run schools a child's knowledge of the Bible would be all-important. Though during the first quarter of the century some of the freedom of the eighteenth century survived, by the mid-Victorian period most middle-class children were subject to a similar discipline. On Sundays, special toys such as the Noah's Ark, a crib, a picture-book of Bible stories, or a picture-block or jigsaw puzzle with religious subjects might have been allowed, but through all these Sunday toys runs the theme of the child being seen, but not heard.

Increase in Mass-produced Toys

Thousands of toy-making firms were established in Europe and America. The German manufacturers had long headed the field in their organization of the toy industry, but they were now more closely followed by the French, with many English firms close behind. They catered for an even wider market and increased their mass-production methods.

It is from the nineteenth century that the collector has to search for his examples. The increasing number of trade marks, and registration of patents, makes it much easier to make attributions of nineteenth-century toys than those of the eighteenth century, which were often estate-made.

A group of toys which the Victorian child would have played with on Sundays, though the painting book might have been frowned on

American Letter
BLOCKS.
FOR WORD
BUILDING
PAINTING BOOK
SUNDAY

The History of Little Fanny, published in 1810 by S. & J. Fuller, gives a paper doll with six costumes and story book, which fit into a pocket-sized wallet

Paper Dolls

Princess Charlotte, as a young lady, sometimes selected her wardrobe by fitting a picture of a dress over a painted portrait. These sheets of costume were popular and, obviously, out-of-date fashions would become playthings. Stout cardboard dolls, made especially for children, had been imported into France from England in the eighteenth century, and these were given an extensive wardrobe. It is, unfortunately, almost impossible to find any early examples of children's paper toys. *The History of Little Fanny* was produced at the beginning of the nineteenth century in several editions and fortunately many survive, but soldiers, ballet dancers and, of course, the much criticized pantins were made before this date.

The value of an old paper doll depends on the condition of the costumes and, obviously, the number of the edition. As they are of all playthings the most fragile, the collector has to look after 1850 to find his examples.

The McLaughlin Brothers of New York published many

attractive paper dolls, among them Topsy, Mrs Tom Thumb, and Commodore Nutte. A Jenny Lind doll, which was very popular, was made in the 1850s and, as is often the case with dolls of this period, the clothes were made double, so they could be slipped over the head. Dolls representing actors, Royal and Holy Families, singers and soldiers, were produced. One portrayed the complete House of Hapsburg including not only the family, but furniture and even towns connected with them!

Women's magazines often included a cut-out boy or girl doll, a custom which is just as popular today. Some firms gave away cut-outs with products such as coffee, dye, crêpe paper or cotton. These advertising dolls can still be found cheaply. It is worth searching through any old magazines for cut-outs which represent the costume of the date of publication, as so few will have survived the hands of an eager child.

Victorian doll advertising thread and 1920s doll cut from an American ladies' magazine of the period

Children's Books

The fact that there is not a great deal of general interest in old children's books does not mean that they can be bought cheaply. For children's books printed before 1800 one must be prepared to possibly spend as much as several hundred pounds because of their rarity, though the one-in-a-million chance of a discovery in the almost mythical junk shop is always possible.

The first book especially aimed at children was the *Kunst und Lehrbüchlein* (1580) with the famous illustration of a boy using a horn book, which was an established part of the

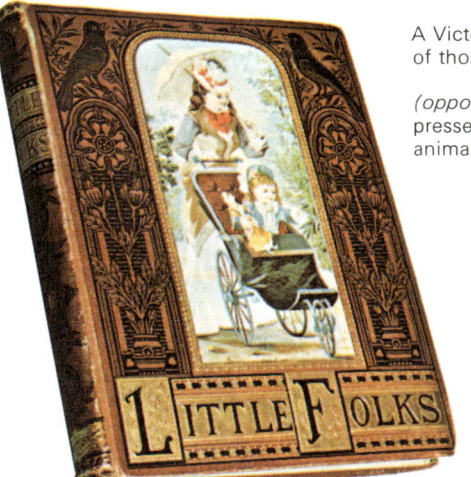

A Victorian picture book typical of those produced after 1860

(opposite) When buttons are pressed the book reproduces animal noises

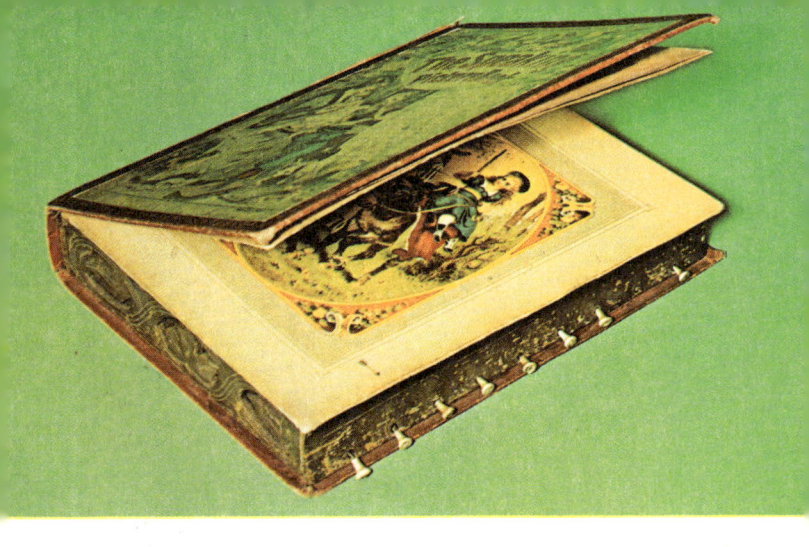

child's equipment. It consisted of a sheet of paper set into a piece of wood with a short handle, the precious parchment protected by a thin layer of horn against the scratching of the pointer used by the child for reading the numbers and letters.

John Locke in 1693 was advocating the use of picture books as the most interesting method of instruction, but as printing was so expensive, only the wealthy child would have owned any. Others would have made use of those primarily written for adults, such as John Bunyan's *Pilgrim's Progress* or John Foxe's *Book of Martyrs*. In books of the period, children were encouraged to lead devout lives, free from earthly pleasure; their ultimate aim should be to die an early and pure death!

Chapmen and Pedlars were circulating much cheaper books by the eighteenth century, which told bloodthirsty and enthralling tales. Unfortunately, being cheaply made and eagerly read, very few of these cheap books have survived. Other, more reasonably priced, bound books were now published, but it was not until John Newbery realized the potential strength of the market that they began to appear in large numbers. His publishing house gave to posterity characters such as Giles Gingerbread and Goody Two-Shoes who appealed more to the child than did the pious works of Hannah More or Mrs Trimmer.

A moving picture book published about 1880 by H. Grevel of Covent Garden

From the start of the eighteenth century there is an ever increasing variety of children's books, and by 1787 the Leipzig Fair had newspapers, plays, journals and almanacs as 'Christmas gifts for good children'.

The nineteenth century is the real field for anyone now wishing to begin a collection. Late Victorian books can still be purchased for a small amount and, even though both the publisher and the author are often rather coy about revealing their identity, these books are often attractive and interesting to read. Many authors still continued the heavenly aspirations of the good ladies of the eighteenth century. Mrs Ewing's *Story of a Short Life* or Mrs Sherwood's *Think before you act* are typical examples. Others begin to exhibit a much lighter approach to life, culminating in such childish fantasies as *The Speaking Picture Book,* which reproduced the noises of birds and animals.

Picture books with shaped covers became very common,

26

and stand-up picture books, which still delight children, were a joy to the Victorian child. Animated books, where umbrellas open and animals move by the pulling of a tab at the side of a page, were all published, especially in Germany. Plays, cut-out dolls, boats and farms were all sold in book form and are rich in colourful detail and period charm, as are the attractively personal scrap books, on which the child lavished so much care.

Annuals became very much part of Christmas, and the cheapness of books made them available to all but the poorest, and ensured a supply for the present-day collector. The price of attractive Victorian and Edwardian books varies. Obviously those which are animated or musical are of more interest than an unnumbered, but pretty, edition of a picture book, and of course, condition is all-important. The works of authors like Kate Greenaway and Florence Upton are especially sought-after, and obviously a complete set increases the value.

Scrap book inscribed 'Gilbert Bridgland from his loving mother 1882'

Educational Toys
Games and Puzzles

The increasing interest of parents in improving the minds of the young, forced the manufacturers into producing toys that commended themselves to the adult, but also attracted the child. Consequently we find many rather tedious games cunningly concealed in boxes, which would have made a direct appeal to the child. Most of the educational toys depended on a card game form, first introduced by Carrington Bowles, Map and Printseller, in 1759, in an edition entitled: *A Journey Through Europe or the Play of Geography*.

Nineteenth-century games are still fairly easy to find. Although it is sometimes difficult to work out quickly whether all the pieces are present, it is advisable to do so, as the value is obviously relative to this. Games which give instruction in biography, religion, heraldry, arithmetic and Shakespeare, are all common. Many are based on the *Happy Families*' principle, and one game taught languages by stand-up characters, which bore on their backs their names in French, German and English.

My Grandmother, a jigsaw puzzle by Mr Upton, published in 1813 by William Darton Jnr

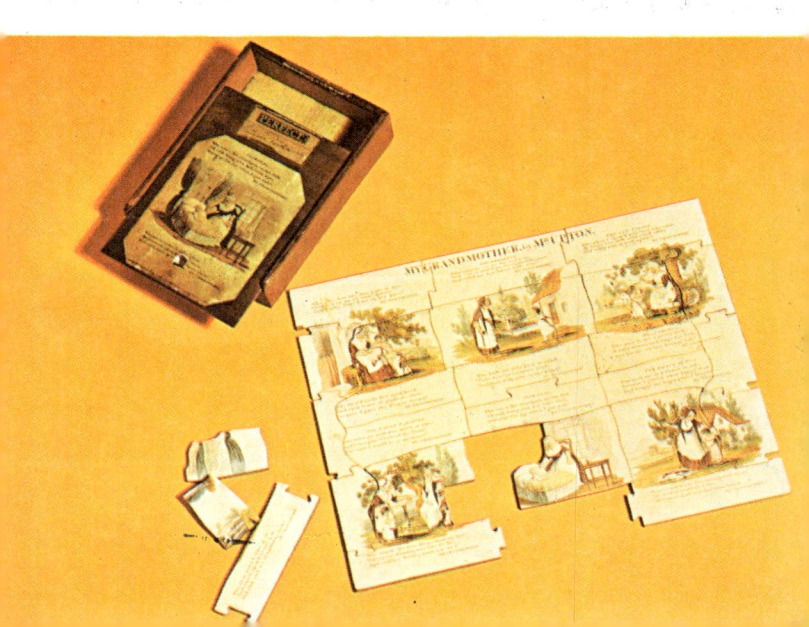

Dissected map of South America published in 1850. Box 18×24 ins. (46×61 cm.)

Games from the Regency period are rarer, but amusing to the adult of today. The game of *Virtue rewarded and Vice Punished,* published in 1818, led the child through a Bunyan-like progress of temptations and pitfalls to reach, if he was lucky, the pure quality of *Virtue*. Many of the early Victorian toys also have this high moral tone, but by the end of the century, adults seem to have given up the effort of buying only improving toys, and much more frivolous products are found.

Early jigsaws are often mounted on mahogany and contained in boxes of the same wood. They were introduced between 1760 and 1770 by Wallis and Son, Mapmakers, and at first depicted stock maps, though later more effort was made to attract the child. One Regency puzzle, with the owner's name

29

A set of late Victorian picture blocks in excellent condition

'Frederick' neatly written on the back, depicts a simple everyday scene, which makes little effort to teach. I feel Frederick may have objected strongly to an irritating puzzle, which was accompanied by a game that could not be played until the puzzle was solved.

The process of lithography, which was introduced in the 1850s in Germany, made colourful toys cheap to produce, and the market was flooded with German products mounted on cheaper softwoods. Construction kits, as well as games, were now introduced, and it would have been much more satisfactory to create a town or fort out of colourful cut-outs with all the accompanying mess of glue and cardboard, than to sit tidily around a table playing a card game like a group of eighteenth-century adults. Model farms, castles, houses and boats could all be constructed from these attractive sheets. By the end of the century, a ship, H.M.S. Blake, made of wood and cardboard to be assembled at home, was given away in exchange for tea coupons, while many others carried advertising material.

Stone building bricks have their origins in antiquity, but they became very popular after they were mass-produced by Richter and Company in the 1880s. They were accompanied by delightful illustrations of the buildings which could be created and, having built several myself, I can vouch for their success!

Alongside wooden and stone building bricks existed more complicated cut-out kits, such as the illustrated *School for Little Builders* produced in Germany, with a neat English title to stick over the German one on export boxes. This game, in which the pieces are joined by strips of tin, calls for extreme skill, as my efforts to build the complete church have been most unsuccessful. The parent is encouraged by the title to imagine he is helping a young architect along his way.

Boys' magazines, which gained an increasing audience, encouraged enthusiasm for chemistry sets, which probably gave as much pleasure to the father as to the child, as did the Meccano and Hornby construction sets, which were produced in the early twentieth century. Many games and kits have survived, but obviously those which make attractive display pieces are most sought after.

An 'educational' card game, about 1880, entitled 'Zooloo'

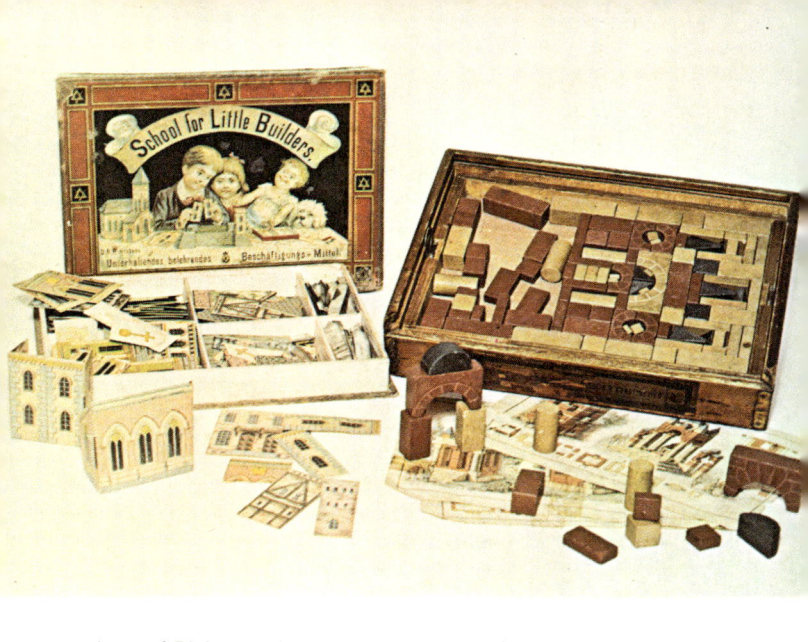

A set of Richter building bricks which the firm introduced in 1883 and a German card and metal construction set, late Victorian

Toys to Teach Domestic Skills

In the grounds of Osborne House, on the Isle of Wight, is a miniature Swiss chalet planned by Prince Albert for the Royal children, where the princesses could learn cooking and baking, and the boys carpentry in a small workshop. The Great Exhibition of 1851, which was so influenced by Albert, had a children's section that was very much directed towards learning skills.

Judging by the number of toy mangles and sewing-machines which still exist, almost every little girl must have owned one of these, or possibly both. The sewing-machines, in particular, are often very decorative and usually work quite satisfactorily. The small tin toy oven, common well into the twentieth century, was heated by a candle placed under the hot-plate, which soon boiled a small saucepan of milk for toy tea parties. A great variety of small metal flat irons on fretted stands were also made, many of which have obviously seen much use, and taught the girl, very early in life, how easy it is to scorch a garment!

Housekeeping in miniature could be assisted by cardboard and metal money. One set bears the head of Prince Albert and the inscription of *H.R.H. Prince Albert P.W.* on the obverse and *12 pence make one shilling* on the reverse. This particular set of coins was made in metal, but sets of cardboard coins are difficult to find in an acceptable state.

All sorts of cleaning utensils were made in miniature, including the buckets, mops and scrubbing-brushes, well known to every kitchen maid. Washday sets were also popular with scrubbing-boards, tubs and clothes-horses to carry the washed and starched dolls' clothes.

Almost every piece of equipment to be found in a Victorian kitchen was made in miniature, some of the cast-iron kitchen ranges, decorated with brass, being more in the line of a fine model than a toy. Lemon-squeezers, coffee-grinders and other small objects abound, and could form in themselves a collection of scope and charm.

The sewing-machine was a popular toy at the end of the nineteenth century, as it taught a useful skill. Most examples still work

Money-boxes

One of life's great virtues for the 'well brought up' Victorian child was the saving of money. Many contemporary stories have references to the worthless spendthrift who fails in life, while his poorer friend, by working hard and putting aside his money, succeeds.

The simple money-boxes of the Middle Ages are virtually impossible to find, though the well-known Piggy Banks, which were popular from the sixteenth century, can occasionally be discovered. The Victorian money-boxes, in whose manufacture the American makers were supreme, were often automated to give some pleasure in saving pocket-money. One such box shows Theodore Roosevelt shooting a bear, whose head emerges from the trunk of a tree, in which he was hiding when shot by the coin.

The Creedmore Bank, where a soldier shoots a coin into a tree-trunk, is more common and, of course, the Jolly Nigger Boy, who sets an unwholesome example by swallowing his

An American money-box, about 1877, known as the 'Creedmore' Bank. This is one of the more commonly found mechanical boxes

Two money-boxes illustrating the variety to be found. *(Right)* A child's tin bagatelle box, made around 1930, and a solid brass bank probably made as a chimney ornament at the end of the last century

pennies, is the most common and most reproduced of all.

An ingenious bulldog responds to a pull on his tail by tossing a coin, previously balanced on his nose, into the air, and catching it in his mouth while waggling his ears! Such unusual boxes are now justifiably fetching high prices.

Many of the Staffordshire potteries produced china money-boxes, particularly in the shape of spaniels' heads and small cottages. Great care should be taken when buying, as vast quantities of reproductions have been made.

Cheap money-boxes, which would have been owned by poor children, can still be bought for well under a pound. They are often decorated with poker work or simple carving and sometimes carry a transfer-printed picture with a small motto. Automated boxes, produced as late as the 1930s, are gaining in interest for collectors as the earlier examples are becoming harder to find.

German tin speedboat, about 1920, powered by burning slug-killer tablets. Thrust is obtained by the expansion of air

Tin Toys
Fine German metal filigree toys have been popular since the eighteenth century, and are still produced today, but tin models did not appear until the early nineteenth century. At first, scrap-metals were used for the making of small objects for dolls' houses and play warfare, the Patterson Brothers of Connecticut being recorded as having made toys of this description. The French were the first to mass-produce pressed tinplate toys and, as new knowledge was gained in the making of low-priced clockwork mechanisms, these were incorporated. French makers also appear to have produced the cheapest toys, though it is difficult to distinguish the country of origin of many of these as they are unmarked and French *émigré* workmen were employed by American makers.

Improving factory techniques made these tin toys very cheap to produce, and simple mechanical toys came within the reach of a great number of children, the mass-production of such toys reaching its peak in the 1880s. Carriages, horses, paddle-steamers, roundabouts, boats and miniature crockery were produced, but are rarely discovered today, so that the new collector has to look among the playthings of the early twentieth century for his purchases. Though it is sometimes possible to find examples of the Lehmann toys, which were made in Germany around the turn of the century, they are very expensive, being probably the most sought-after of the tin toys.

Fortunately, as yet, these small tin toys do not appear to have been reproduced, though I have seen quantities of modern German filigree miniatures being sold as nineteenth-century in the London street markets.

In the early twentieth century, the field is widened by the attractive tins made in the form of toys which were used as advertisements, such as Huntley and Palmer's grandfather clock in *chinoiserie* style, a toy doll's pram, or the splendid Jacob's coronation coach of 1937, all of which were intended as toys once the contents had been eaten.

Express transport delivery van with simple clockwork mechanism, made in England about 1925

The 'Penny Toys'

The description 'Penny Toy' has become a collector's term in classifying the tin models, usually under $3\frac{1}{2}$ ins. (9 cm.) high, which were so popular around the turn of the century. Many of the toys so classified cost considerably more than a single penny, but were sufficiently cheap to be purchased with the few pence given to a child as pocket-money.

The London Museum has a fine collection of some 1,600 different penny toys given by Mr Ernest King, who bought them over sixty years ago from street hawkers near Ludgate Hill. These include aeroplanes, balloons, fire-engines, roundabouts and small models of people at work, such as knife-grinders. All are objects of current interest which would have attracted a boy keeping up-to-date with changes in the world around him.

The paper litho technique, which was introduced in 1895, was often used in decorating the penny toys, though many

These 'Penny Toys' from the London Museum reflect the increasing variety of vehicles to be found in city streets. The model fire engine, in particular, would be a desirable acquisition

To satisfy the child's urge to be up-to-date with engineering advances, 'Penny Toys' which were models of flying machines, real and imaginary, were produced in great numbers

continued to be hand-coloured as they had been throughout the century. Most of these toys were made in Germany, but obviously some were made in other countries. They are particularly collectable, as they do not take up a great deal of space and form a colourful group, though the lack of marked examples makes them difficult to attribute. The detail, and mechanical ingenuity displayed in the manufacture of these toys, makes it surprising that they were sold for so little.

From the beginning of the twentieth century tin toys cease to be at all retrospective and are obviously aimed at keeping up with developments in transport, as the child was no longer satisfied with an old-fashioned vehicle, so that by 1913 there were on sale tin aircraft, some actually powered by compressed air!

An early primitive wooden pull-along train whose construction would suggest little acquaintance with actual railways, about 1845

Trains

The history of the toy train goes back to the crudely made, painted wooden trains with carriages, which were sold with a length of wooden track. These were made in Germany from the advent of the steam train during the first half of the nineteenth century. Some of the early models are so badly made, that the probability of the maker never actually having seen a train is apparent.

During the 1870s, well-made wooden engines were produced alongside metal models, which were made mainly in Germany, often for exporters; they sometimes have English names such as *'The Stephenson'* written on their sides. A train of this type is in the London Museum, while another cheaply made train of around 1840 has a clockwork mechanism. These early trains were sold in attractive boxes, and many came from Nuremberg, though the Americans produced excellent cast-iron trains together with trackless tin pull-alongs.

Toy catalogues from the end of the century show a tremendous variety of accessories; gas lamps, stations in both the Gothic and classical style, bridges and station staff were all included, so that a really effective layout could have been created.

During the nineteenth century, scale remained completely unimportant and was not rationalized, even to the extent of a standard gauge, until after the turn of the century. All the toy trains made before the 1890s appear to have been of coarse scale. The terms *coarse scale* and *fine scale* are used by collectors to indicate adherence by the manufacturer to a true relationship between the gauge of the track, the size of the engine and the size of rolling stock.

Originally the engines were often sold by scientific instrument-makers, and early examples can be recognized by their fine handmade parts and their complete disregard of proportion.

One of the major manufacturers of early model railways was

Model train (gauge one) made in Nuremberg by Bing, about 1905. Bing marked their products G.B.N., standing for 'Gebrüder Bing Nürnberg'

A Hornby clockwork train set made in the 1930s with a few more recent additions. Most Hornby 'O' gauge equipment can still be bought cheaply

the German firm of Märklin, in whose products a collector might trace not only the development of the concept of scale, but also the history of the railways, as they have been active from the 1860s to the present time.

Possibly the most sought-after of English model railways are the products of the firm of Bassett-Lowke, certain of whose models, such as the *'Black Prince'*, almost transcend the field of toys. These were collectors' pieces even in their own day and compare very favourably with models produced currently.

The Ives locomotives, which were made in America, are the most eagerly collected, as so few have survived. As with Bassett-Lowke, the work on many of these little Victorian trains is so fine, that they should really be classed as models rather than toys, especially as they were expensive when new and sufficiently dangerous to make parents nervous of allowing their children to play with them unsupervized, this probably being the origin of the train as father's toy.

Other manufacturers whose products should form part of a collection are Hornby of England, Bing of Germany, and Lionel of America, although pre-1930 examples are increasingly hard to find, especially in an acceptable condition. The products of these firms, certainly until the introduction of electrification, all have a charming disregard for scale and could in no sense be anything other than toys.

Electric railways which were first introduced between the world wars were initially run by batteries, and when the unreliable nature of the power-supply and the small engines is considered, it is not surprising that the clockwork engine retained its popularity for a long period. It is still easy to find Hornby trains of the 1920s and 30s in fairly good condition, and they are an inexpensive starting-point for a new collector.

An example of the work of one of the best-known British model makers, Bassett-Lowke. The locomotive is an Ivatt Class CI Large Boiler Atlantic, made between 1928 and 1932

A carved wooden model of a hussar, made around 1830, which was originally mounted on wheels. About 7 ins. (18 cm.) high

Soldiers

The margin between model and toy is probably more tenuous in the field of military miniatures than in any other aspect of toy collecting. Fine models of warriors are known from the Egyptian tombs, where they were taken to be used in the after-life. During the seventeenth century, playing with model armies and planning sieges was almost a social accomplishment, but it is not until the eighteenth century that genuine metal toy soldiers emerge.

Wooden soldiers, made simply on a lathe and painted, were made universally, sometimes achieving a good degree of realism, while at other times being mere painted skittle shapes.

The Italian miniaturists, Emanuele and Emilio Gin, painted model carboard figures in fine detail for the court of Naples, but simpler paper soldiers were played with from the mid-eighteenth century. Seyfried of Strasbourg sold the first commercially produced examples in 1774 and established Strasbourg as the main paper soldier making centre. They were later rivalled by the wood-block prints from Epinal in the Vosges, where the Pellerin brothers produced sheets of printed soldiers which were coloured by hand.

Various composition substances have been used for the construction of miniature figures, such as the product marketed in 1936 under the trade name of *Elastolin*. Where a composition substance is used, the figures tend to be rather large and obviously toys.

The making of toy soldiers became a craft industry – not only in Germany but also in Switzerland and France – encouraged at the end of the eighteenth century by the creation of inexpensive alloys, which put metal objects within the reach of ordinary people. The increasing standardization of army uniforms worn by professional soldiers led to boys identifying themselves to a greater extent with the models

A small group of Britain's model soldiers made before 1938. The fort, which is Bavarian, dates from 1925

Flat-backed lead German infantry and military band, about 1895.
A type of model made almost continuously until the First World War

with which they played, alongside model drums, flags and the attractive miniature uniforms which they sometimes wore themselves.

Collecting model soldiers was a popular adult craze by the end of the nineteenth century, so much so, that a Parisian shopkeeper manufactured some mock medieval figures and pretended to recover them from the Seine. The interest is not surprising, as the eighteenth-century flat-backed lead soldiers, made by the firm of Hilpert at Nuremberg, are extremely fine, and collectors at the turn of the century were eager to find actual medieval examples to augment their range.

Hilpert moved to Nuremberg in 1750 and was succeeded by other members of his family. Together with the Heinrichsens and Allgeyer, he made Nuremberg the world centre for metal toy soldiers. Their families established the Nuremberg scale for models – being a height of 30 mm. for foot and 40 mm. for mounted soldiers – though not all makers fell in line. Early Hilpert models are marked *A.H.*, or even carry the full name of the firm. The figures were sold unpainted and by weight, in oval boxes, which contained from 20-150 soldiers.

Lucotte, a Parisian metal-worker, is usually considered to have been the first to produce figures in the round, in French army uniforms, around 1789, but by 1850 Cuberly, Blondel and Gerbeau provided competition, selling their products in very ornate boxes, with the trademark CBG, which is still used.

William Britain introduced changes in manufacture around 1890, which considerably lowered the price of models, as hollow figures could now be made. After the amalgamation of the firm with Herald Miniatures, Britains considerably increased their range of uniformed soldiers and also added fox-hunting groups, station figures, etc. Britains went on producing metal figures until quite recently, and odd figures can still be bought for a few pence.

The Golden Age of the Nuremberg soldiers ceased with the Treaty of Versailles, which had prohibited the making of military emblems in Germany. Surviving examples are very scarce, though often augmented by modern casts of early models.

A wooden German fort with detail on lithographed paper, about 1890, with small soldiers mainly made in France

German 'Kindertheater' published by J. F. Schreiber between 1870 and 1920. The realistic sets reflected the theatrical fashion

Toy Theatres

Melodrama, with its accompanying exaggerated emotions and movements, lent itself well to a paper representation, and the engravers further improved on nature, so that the cut-out actors have a vigour that is attractively grotesque.

The Augsburg printers issued plays in the eighteenth century, as did the Viennese, but the English model theatre progressed from the engraved sheets, which carried the representations of a few actors, and were sold as adult souvenirs around 1811. J. H. Jameson quickly marketed plays especially for children, with lighting equipment, curtains, and slides for positioning the actors.

It is not known for sure whether the claim to be: 'The Original Inventor and Publisher of Juvenile Theatrical Prints, Established 1808', made by J. K. Green was strictly true, as William West had produced some earlier examples, but it was certainly J. K. Green who first sold both plain and coloured versions. Firms such as R. Lloyd, Hodgson and Company, and J. H. Jameson were also issuing plays, but were overshadowed by the cheaper range of Matthew Skelt.

The toy theatre is now synonymous with the name of Pollocks, which still sell reprints of the theatrical sets that were sold by John Reddington in the 1850s. Plays such as *The Grand Melodrama of the Broken Sword* had pocket-money buyers, though Hodgson's *Zoroaster* cost the large sum of 29/6d. in the coloured version.

As plays were so often re-issued, they are not easy to date, and few theatres have survived complete. Modern reprints sold by Pollocks are often to be found under the guise of Victorian models, having been given a coat of yellow varnish, but examination of the wooden structure soon reveals the forger's carelessness.

William West probably published this impressive proscenium front. Webb's backdrop is from the harlequinade, 'Jack and the Beanstalk'

The *Zoëtrope*, or 'wheel of life', was patented in Britain in 1860. When the drum was revolved, a number of spectators could glimpse the flickering figures in apparent motion through slits in the drum

Optical Toys

The children of the Duchess of Devonshire were said to have been instructed by an early magic lantern in the eighteenth century, but these devices really came into their own in the late nineteenth century, when they were cheaply produced in America, Germany and France. Some of the early decorative lanterns are very attractive, though the slides themselves are more fascinating than the most complicated *Panoptique*, a refinement which could also project pictures cut from magazines.

Many slides are skilfully hand-painted by artists such as Joseph Aubert of Paris. The slides which accompany the lantern are interesting, as although some are dated 1922, the designs are still in the high Victorian tradition.

A strong religious or instructive theme runs through many of the nineteenth-century optical toys, though the *Thaumo-*

trope, where a disc is quickly revolved, so that the figures presented separately on either side become united, was usually designed purely to amuse.

The *Zoëtrope*, which was very popular, consisted of a sheet of paper on which were drawn figures in the stages of movement. The paper was placed in a hollow cylinder with slits cut in the sides, so that when spun, the images seen through the apertures gave the illusion of movement. The fascination with the phenomenon of the persistence of vision led to such inventions as the *Kinetoscope*, from which the cinema film of today was developed.

Many optical toys, such as the Tri-Unial lantern, which could effect dissolving and fading views, were aimed at the adult market and would probably have been operated with enthusiasm by the father, rather than the child.

The stereoscopic card-viewer, giving a three-dimensional effect, was a popular Victorian parlour toy. The magic lantern could project simple glass slides or rackwork slides animated by cranking a handle

Late nineteenth-century Bavarian farm stocked with the type of mass-produced wooden animals more commonly found in Noah's Arks

Toy Farms and Noah's Arks

The German toy-makers' method of dividing up work, made economic the large number of animals which could be included in an ark. A woman might learn to carve six different animals and simply repeat these for her whole life. An article from *Playthings* (1897) states: 'In one house they will perhaps do nothing but paint grey horses with black spots in another only red horses with white spots.' This mass manufacture on a folk basis made the toys cheap, as they were first cut in outline on the lathe, and then sliced into segments, so that only the carved finish was worked by hand.

The ark was known as a toy as early as 1642, and believed to have been first made at Oberammergau in Germany. Toy farms were made alongside arks. The similarity between the animals on the illustrated farm and those found usually in arks is obvious. Fewer farms are to be found in England than arks, the illustrated example having been brought into the country by a German family in the 1930s.

The arks range from 12-36 ins. (30-90 cm.) in length, with cheaper versions simply standing on a flat board. Late in the nineteenth century a decorative lithographed finish is often seen. The Gothic windows and doors which were so often added, make them look like churches. My father inherited an ark which had an unusual ratchet system, by which the animals entered, while Noah stood noting them down in his book.

The illustrated ark is a pure 'Sunday Toy'. The heavy wooden base has iron wheels to facilitate movement. The attempted realism of the rudder is amusing, as is the belled cat, which accords strangely with the Old Testament costume of the main characters. The number of animals has been depleted by the fragile nature of the composition substance, which breaks off the wire armature, if roughly handled.

This Noah's Ark is very much a Sunday toy with its realistic crib-like figures. Nineteenth-century, made of composition similar to Elastolin

Toy Horses and Carts

Horse-drawn transport of a period has always been reflected in toys, from a simple terracotta chariot horse, to the water-carriers of the nineteenth century, which kept the dust in city streets down to a minimum.

Many of the horses appear to have been made in one area, or by one firm, as in many nineteenth-century examples from England the same horse, only in different sizes, is seen attached to a farm cart or delivery van, often with little regard for proportion. The horses usually stand singly on bases, though occasionally in pairs, being very simply made and crudely painted. In contrast, the carts are often very beautifully made and carry imaginary inscriptions such as: *'Derby and Bright – Coal Merchants – Best Wallsend Coal'*, or *'Fresh Milk – Thistle Farm'*.

The fine large brewer's dray which is illustrated, was made in 1850 for the son of a brewer from Essex, the horse being carved in the town of Coggeshall, which was famed for its

An estate-made brewer's dray which has been in the possession of the Gardiner family of Coggeshall for a hundred-and-twenty years

A crudely made nineteenth-century hay-cart with its price of 7/6d underneath. Driven by jointed S.P.B.H. doll

woodcarvers. The dray was made by the brewery carpenter, who has included detail never found on commercially made examples. It has survived several generations of children intact, except for a few barrels. Such estate-made examples occur in most spheres of toy collecting and are interesting, as they are well documented, which is far from the case with commercial examples. I have not to date found any made before 1900 with a maker's mark or any indication of origin.

Wooden horses were made in the Italian Alps, but these are slimmer than the English toy and often wear a painted blanket. English- or American-made carts are sometimes attached to them, but the partnership is never very successful. The carts have frequently been repainted and stripping them down to their original paint, with a thin piece of glass, is really a labour of love!

Well carved horses, sometimes in pairs, one rearing and the other perhaps turning its head, were made during the Regency period and often appear in illustrations of the time. For example, in a water-colour of the salon of the Wittgenstein family at Ivanovskij, which is in the collection of Don Agostino Chigi in Rome, a boy drags a similar pair of wheeled horses across the floor, encouraging them with a miniature whip. Another finely carved horse of the 1830s was owned by the children of Francesco I, King of Naples. This steed wore a garland of flowers around its neck and a fine embroidered blanket, and was of the high quality that one expects of a prince's toy.

Ordinary children bought their horses from country fairs, or from city toyshops, such as the illustrated push-along horse from Hamleys toyshop in London. The name of the toyshop is written on a plate on the green base, but often the names have been painted over, or become rusty. This type of horse also tends to have lost much of its gesso, and is not usually in this excellent original condition.

Large wooden horse on spring rockers which still wears its original brass marked: 'G. & J. L. London'. Made by Lines Brothers, about 1895

A push-along painted wooden horse marked with its seller's name, 'Hamleys'. Edwardian, and *(right)* a pull-along skin-covered horse, about 1880

The rocking-horse changed its form at the end of the century, and was suspended by 'safety rocks', the traditional curved variety often leading to falls. Lines Brothers, the leading British maker, made horses in a wide variety of sizes, up to the life-sized versions used by tailors. Among their productions were: 'Best Cart Horses' at 3/- to 11/6d., and large rocking-horses at '83/- best quality'. Mr W. Lines remembers how the horses were made during the spring, and stored until near Christmas, when they were given two coats of zinc-white and one of grey, and spotted.

Edwardian horses are often very ingenious, having mechanisms which enable the skin-covered horse to be both a wheeled push-along and a rocking-horse; this type was a favourite prop for photographers, and is often found in old albums.

As the child pulled along this toy by its string, the two figures rocked in the swing-boat. English, about 1800

Wheeled Toys

Donkeys carrying panniers and standing on a wheeled base were very popular from the eighteenth century, as the panniers could be used to carry other small toys. Unusual examples of wheeled toys are sometimes found, such as the illustrated swinging boat, which was owned by a town clerk of Colchester. The two figures pull on ropes as the swing is dragged along the ground, causing the composition dolls to be swung realistically. The Holly Trees Museum in Colchester also has a fine hussar which was originally on wheels, and is about 7 ins. (18 cm.) high (see page 44).

Maria Edgeworth, the nineteenth-century novelist, describes

how in 'A Rational Toy Shop' of the 1860s traps and coaches were sold without horses, the child himself becoming the horse and beating his bottom as he trotted along. In this type of shop were to be found sensible toys, such as wheelbarrows, rather than the model animals which were bought by unenlightened parents. To a collector, however, it is probably the purchases of the less progressive parents which are the more interesting.

The baby-walker is not the new aid that the mothercraft books would have us believe, being frequently shown in Continental paintings from the sixteenth century. Miniature

A dipped wax doll which swings its legs on a wire rod as the baby-walker is moved along. Made about 1880

walkers were made for dolls such as the one illustrated, which is swinging its legs to simulate walking as it moves along.

The disadvantage of many of the wheeled toys is their size, as four or five of them can occupy a complete wall of an average house. Fortunately, their making involves too much work for reproduction, and their price is comparatively low, as they are usually collected only by the most enthusiastic, or by doll collectors who wish to use them for the display of the dolls themselves. Small toys, such as the illustrated examples, are much more desirable to the general collector of toys, particularly as they are both automated.

From about 1870, there was a wider variety of materials from which wheeled toys could be made commercially. A thick cardboard substance covered with horse-skin was particularly popular and very effective when new. Now, however, it sometimes looks macabre, especially on the larger wooden rocking-horses, as recovering is never very successful.

Fine leather was often used to give a realistic effect on the shape of toys made of pressed cardboard, such as the elephant and camel which are illustrated. It was no longer sufficient for a toy to stand stiffly and be pulled along, so the camel croaks when a cord is pulled and the elephant nods his head lugubriously as he is moved along.

A papier-mâché mixture, covered with flocking powder,

Two pull-along skin-covered animals, about 1880. The elephant nods its head and the camel croaks when a string in the neck is pulled

Papier-mâché French bulldog, about 1890, whose head nods when he is pulled along on hidden wheels, and when the lead is pulled he barks

was used extensively, particularly on the Barking Bulldogs, which have survived in some variety. An English Bulldog made in a similar way to the dog illustrated, stands about 1 ft. (30 cm.) high, but much larger dogs were made; one, nearly full life-size, wears a collar bearing the words: 'Bulldog Mascot', which would lead to the supposition that these dogs were often sold for adults rather than children. They are now popular as drawing-room conversation pieces, many times being purchased by people with no interest in other antique toys.

When clockwork mechanisms became cheap, they were often used to propel the wheeled toys, and tricycles, dolls' pushing prams, trams and trains are found. The flywheel was often used as a lighter alternative to clockwork, and was often given a ratchet-start device on small toys. Most of the old clockwork toys tend to be very expensive if in good condition and are difficult to restore if rusted; consequently the new

Victorian corrugated metal dolls' pram with brass and china decoration to handle and hood. 'Melita' doll, 1910

collector has to take most of his examples from the twentieth century.

Dolls' Prams
The forerunner of the toy pram was a simple wicker cradle with a hood, which was sometimes pulled along by string, but more often, especially when large, pushed by a wooden handle on a bar. A similar toy is seen in a water-colour of 1839, but the wicker has now been replaced by a wooden frame.

Prams developed along the same lines in Europe and America, and by 1875 had become a wheelbarrow-like shape, with two large spider wheels at the back and one small wheel at the front. This type was usually very well finished, having china handles and decoratively painted coachwork, the interior often deeply buttoned either in leather or an imitation. The handle is always behind the head of the doll, which is facing away from the child pushing the pram along. As this type of pram continued to be made into the twentieth century, it is advisable to examine the construction well before establishing a date.

Mail carts in a variety of sizes were popular from the 1880s, Simpson, Fawcett and Co. advertising them as 'useful for developing the physique and improving the health'. The small version of the toy had a basket-seat in which the doll sat. Mail carts were made in thousands, and can still be found quite easily, but though they made excellent toys having a wide variety of uses, they are not very satisfactory for the display of dolls.

The pram developed into its full splendour by the end of the century. The hood which had often been a simple umbrella-like device, now resembled the modern pram hood and could be collapsed, and the doll now sat facing the child who was pushing the pram along. Wickerwork was often used most

Edwardian wooden pram. The deep sides added to the shallow base of an earlier model, to keep in line with changing fashion. 'C.P.' doll

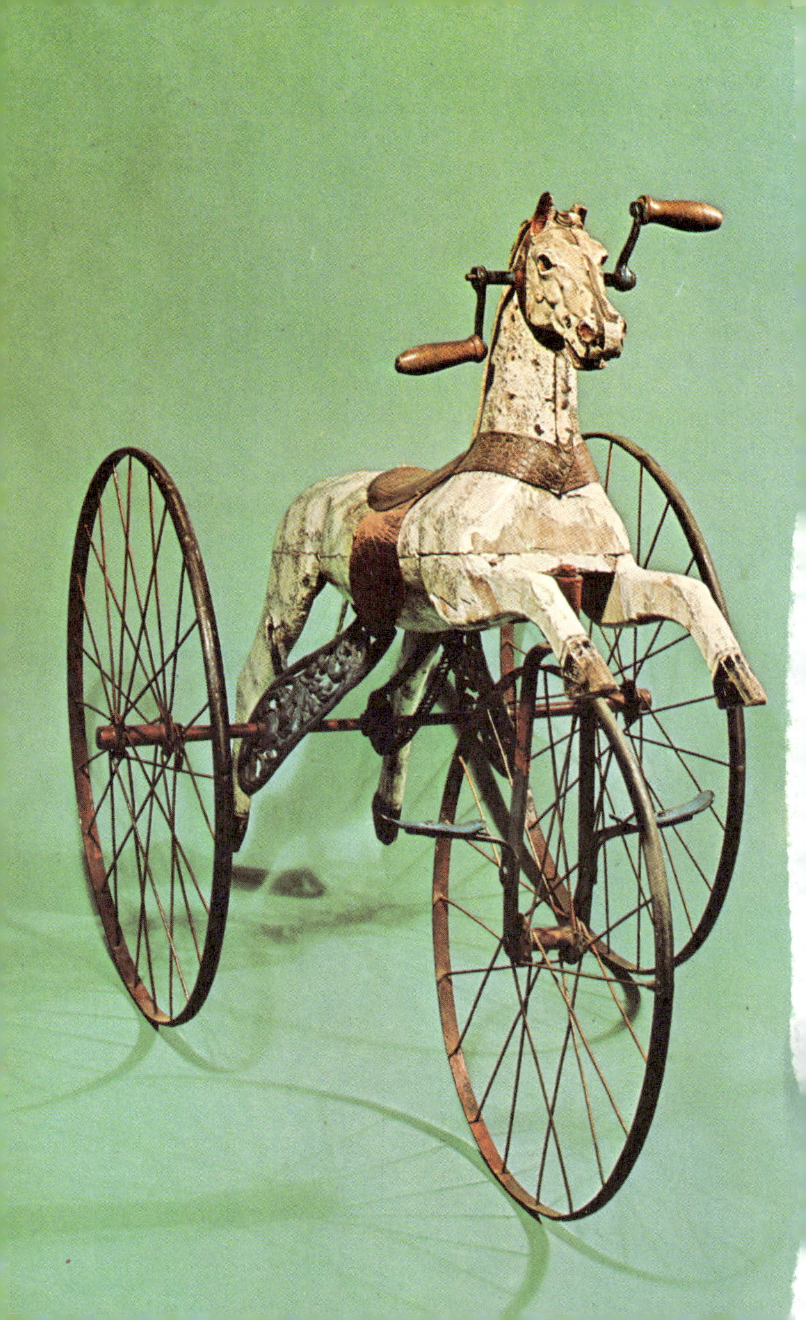

attractively in the manufacture, but many prams have been spoiled by continual repainting, the wooden ones usually having stayed in better condition.

Tricycles and Scooters

The first mentioned toy transport was the self-propelled go-cart of 1822, but the *velocipede* horse, basically a tricycle with a horse's body, is seen as early as 1853 in the nursery of a young prince. Early velocipedes have a slim, rather unrealistic, body, often covered with ponyskin, with a great deal of decorative cast ironwork on the tricycle frame. The horse is usually made of wood, though the head is sometimes of metal. They are usually propelled by pedals, sometimes with the assistance of a chain-drive mechanism. Edwardian velocipedes are more like plump rocking-horses, and were sold either with spider or rubber wheels. With glass eyes and padded saddles, they cost around £2, though one advertiser in the *Bazaar* of 1889 offered a fine second-hand one for sale at £1!

G. Townend of Coventry advertised themselves as 'The Original Juvenile Tricycle Manufacturers' and their 1883 catalogue shows a particularly elegant two-seater tricycle, the two seats being side by side with upright bars for steering. Early versions all have the upright bars on either side of the rider, which enabled the large wheeled toy to be steered, but by 1905 the tricycle is seen in its basic modern form with handlebars, alongside the child's pennyfarthing.

The scooter also became popular as a toy in the early years of this century, often having two additional small wheels at the back to act as a brake. The scooter is never found with the excessive decoration sometimes found on tricycles, as functionalism was rearing its plain head. There is at present a fashion for burnishing the finely shaped toys, which is sad from the collector's point of view, though the process does reveal the detail of many examples and makes them attractive to interior decorators.

Fine *velocipede* horse from Penshurst Place Toy Museum, propelled by handles on the head and steered by the feet. A popular toy, though few have survived due to their size. About 1850

Wooden Edwardian rocking-boat. Probably estate-made for the children of a Welsh ironmaster. Large Kestner and Rauenstein dolls

Rocking-boats and Toy Cars

The see-saw in its most basic form is seen all over the world, but in the nineteenth century it is found in its most splendid guise. See-saws often had small chairs fitted on either side of a rocking base, sometimes with safety bars to protect the child. These wooden chairs on rockers were made well into the twentieth century, many of the simplest versions being found in schools.

The same rocking principle is seen in boats which were used as carpet toys in large houses. They are usually very well finished, though they appear to have been estate-made, as were many Edwardian toy cars.

Toy pedal cars originated probably in America, but they were quickly produced in Europe, some being poorly finished, as they were obviously home-made. Lines Brothers were producing cars at the beginning of the century, and followed closely the advances in design. The cars were made both in wood and metal, and one even in basketwork!

The more expensive cars were large. Some had a great deal of realistic detail and seated up to four children, as did some of the large pedal trains. It was possible to hire these cars and trains at the seaside and they are often seen in old photographs, being driven along the promenade.

Memories of my infant school in the 40s are haunted by a Genevieve-type car, which stood roped off from the toy-hungry hands of the children. The school had also inherited a roomful of Edwardian toys, but we were never allowed near the velocipedes, trains and cars that were temptingly displayed around us. A few years ago I asked permission to photograph some of these treasures, only to be told that they had been broken up – all that remained was the rocking-boat which is illustrated.

Splendid Edwardian child's car (Renault model) from The Museum of Childhood, Edinburgh. Probably estate-made

Asalto board which can also be used for solitaire, c. 1880

Board Games

The Royal Game of Goose reputedly came into Europe from Greece at the end of the sixteenth century. From this game, which involves the negotiation of a circular board, are evolved all the eighteenth- and nineteenth-century board games.

France, in particular, produced many variations and the Abbé Gaultier, who was a refugee from the French Revolution, is said to have invented many of the moral and instructive games that English and American children played with. The adult love of gaming made a child quickly familiar with dice and cards, one famous lady blaming her parents for her subsequent disgrace, as they had taught her the love of gaming at a tender age.

J. Harris of London published in 1809 an attractive game: 'A Days Journey Around the Metropolis Depicting 50 Places to Visit in London.' The firm gave itself some advertising space in the game by the inclusion of an illustration of their shop at 'The Juvenile Library, Corner of St Paul's Churchyard'.

A game called: *'The Magic Ring'*, which took the child on an enchanted journey through Fairyland, is a refreshing change from most of the board games that are often extremely boring, despite their very attractively decorated surfaces.

Chess, draughts and solitaire, though actually adult games, have long been played by children. Versions of these games aimed at the juvenile market are extremely difficult to find, as they have usually lost their original boxes which were probably all that differentiated them from adult versions. Chess pieces are collected in their own right and are often extremely beautiful. These games are refreshing, as they do not attempt to moralize or impart useless knowledge but as games of skill have ensured their continual popularity.

Two late nineteenth-century table games intended to amuse and instruct. 'Fishponds', is a parlour game for four persons. English, about 1890. 'Meteor Ball Mosaic Game No. 7', made by Richter & Cie., Rudolstadt, Germany, is a game for making patterns with coloured balls

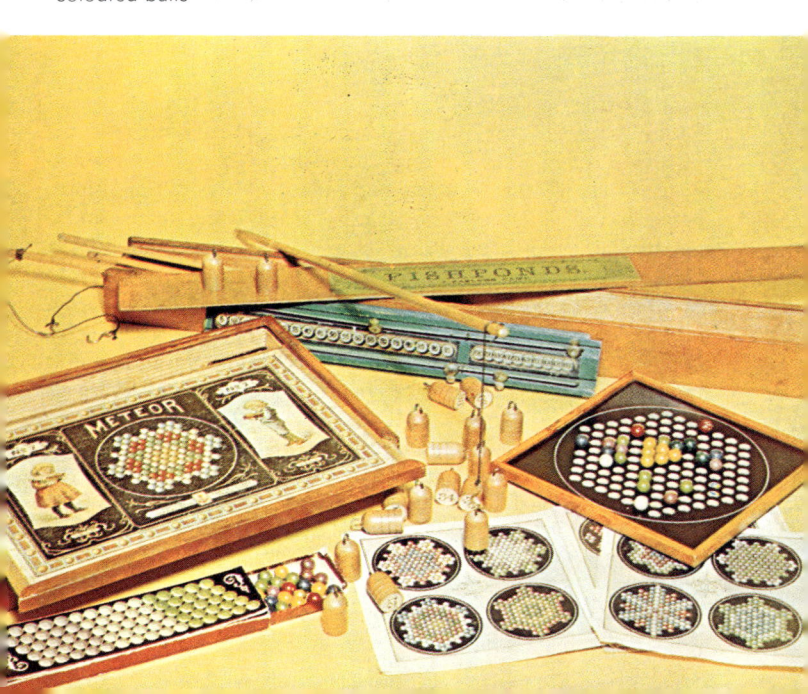

Though butcher's shops are recognized as particularly English toys, some were manufactured in Germany for sale in England. About 1880

Toy Shops

Practically every toy museum has a model of a nineteenth-century butcher's shop, a type of toy shop which has survived well, as most of the contents were made of wood. Sometimes the shop was made most realistically, with living accommodation upstairs, complete with royal coat-of-arms and potted plants. Many toy shops, such as the one illustrated, are merely interiors in boxes. All the joints of meat, rabbits and poultry unhook for sale, and the sawdust-covered floors are realistically bloodstained. The similarity between many examples would suggest that they could have been made by the same firm or craftsman.

Grocers' shops were also an educational aid, though the tin scales in many versions are hardly accurate. There is a great variety of standard, many having been home-made and stocked with miniature advertising samples, whose distribution had spread from America. The 1930s shop illustrated is a cheap version and commercially made, carrying a wealth of advertising material that cunningly acquainted the child with the packaging of certain products at an early age.

Dress shops and milliners' are more frivolous, and they often exhibit some beautifully made miniature dresses and hats. One shop I have long coveted is staffed by four French fashion dolls, who offer for sale dresses, and fine hats in boxes.

The value of a shop depends on its number of wares. An empty grocer's shop is very difficult to stock and though it is easy to make loaves of bread, miniature jellies and packets, this would be unsatisfactory to a toy collector.

Shops of the 1920s and 30s can still be purchased cheaply, as long-established collectors are not yet interested in them. The illustrated shop cost only £2 in a London antique market a few months ago.

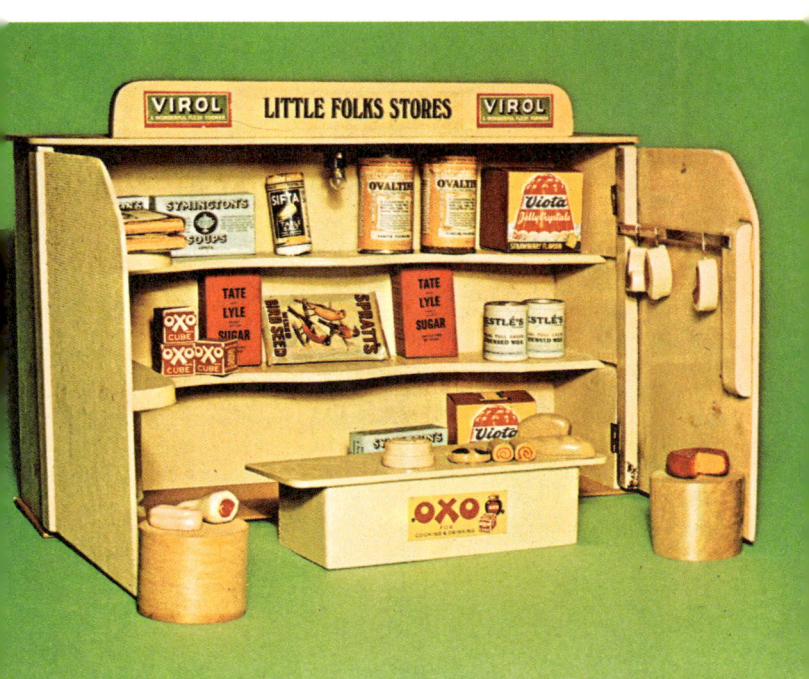

A grocer's shop, made around 1930, stocked with advertising samples of popular products. Toys of this vintage can still be bought cheaply *(left)* Chest-of-drawers, apprentice piece, about 1890 and *(right)* early nineteenth-century dresser, 11 ins. (28 cm.) high. Well made, but not of the standard of an apprentice piece. The carved panels on the doors are unusually good for a toy. The china is mass-produced, nineteenth-century, German. This type of china often has decoration similar to that produced by the Meissen factory

Miniature Furniture

The term 'miniature furniture' usually refers to pieces that are too large for a dolls' house. There is a great disparity of finish between examples, some, no doubt, having been roughly put together by an indulgent parent. Very fine examples are often referred to as 'travellers' samples' or 'apprentice pieces'. The idea of an apprentice finishing off his training by making one excellent miniature model rests mainly on tradition. It is more likely that most of the models were made for sheer pleasure, rather in the way that glass-makers made small glass articles, known as 'friggers'. The ordering of such a frivolity might also have appealed to the fancy, and, in the case of coffers and chests of drawers, have been useful for storing trinkets.

It is also unlikely that these small pieces of furniture could have been the 'models at large' so often recommended by Chippendale for the practice of difficult undertakings, as the models reflect ordinary fashion in furniture. Many pieces were intended purely as toys, such as a fine, banded slant-top desk, complete with escutcheons, whose label reads: 'New Toy Shop/in Arch Street, three doors below Fifth Street,/ Philadelphia./A handsome assortment of English and German Toys just opened and for sale, Wholesale and/Retail, cheap for Cash or short Credit/Abraham Forst 1816.' The Tower Toy Guild, which was formed by a group of American craftsmen, produced some fine carved grandfather clocks, settles, Windsor chairs and cradles. As many miniature pieces were marked only with a stuck-on label it is not surprising, that like ordinary furniture, they are difficult to identify. Many small coffers have initials carved on them, but these could have belonged either to the owner or the maker.

The fine quality highboys, commodes, sideboards and sofas, if made before 1850, are extremely rare, but late Victorian and Edwardian examples, which are often more obviously toys, are still within the average collector's range.

A group of fine craftsman-made miniature items constructed by the upholsterer to Queen Victoria. Good quality miniature items rather than children's toys, of the mid-nineteenth century

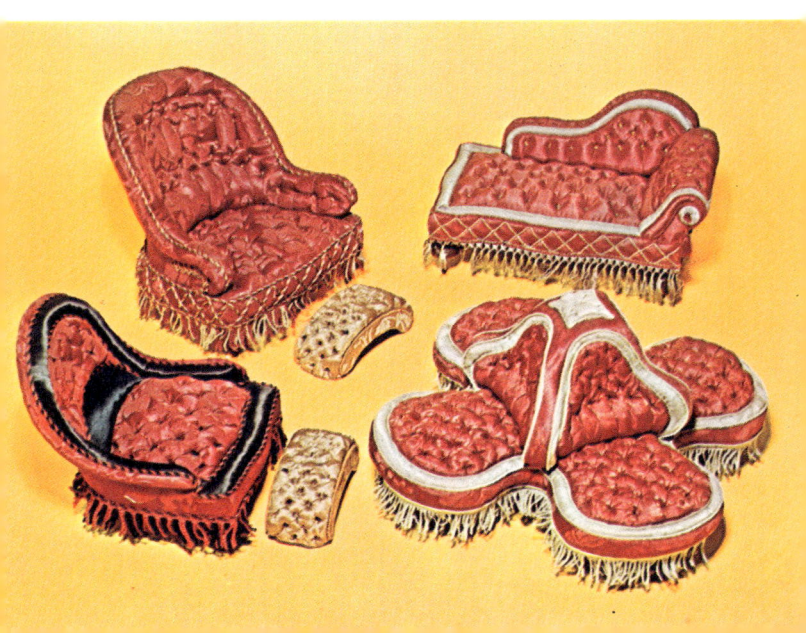

Mid-nineteenth-century German miniature dinner service with painted decoration of birds. Each piece has a different design

Toy China

Crudely made miniature mugs and pitchers are to be found among the relics of early civilization in most countries, and are still fairly inexpensive to buy as they are not collected generally, being mainly of interest to museums. Over most early European well-made miniature china there is the controversy as to its intention – travellers' samples or toys? As the miniature dinner services were often composed of up to one hundred pieces, and would have been made from special moulds with scaled-down transfer prints, it seems unlikely that a factory would have wasted time making them as travellers' samples.

Some of the early English pottery, such as that made at Leeds at the end of the eighteenth century, seems too lovely ever to have been played with, but its presence in Baby Houses of the date suggest that this was so, especially as small pieces are sometimes found with food moulded onto the plate, such as a pair of cauliflowers, or fish garnished with lemon slices.

Early Wedgwood miniature sets are much sought after, as is the 'Young Nankeen' referred to by Mrs Mary Delany, the eighteenth-century autobiographer, and which was probably made in Caughley or Lowestoft, where extremely lovely services, often in the *chinoiserie* style, were produced.

After about 1850, there is a wealth of material from which to select a sphere of collecting, as cheap china sets were imported from Germany and, together with the earthenware sets produced by the English potteries, offered an inexpensive range. All sorts of scenes are shown on the pieces, from children flying kites, to patterns which are obvious cut-downs of transfers that were used on larger sets.

German sets, which are often very attractive, though unmarked, are still to be found quite easily, though marked English examples, with an acceptable number of pieces, are becoming more difficult to discover. Individual pieces are still not expensive, and an attractive collection could be made of perhaps just plates, or cups and saucers, produced by various factories.

English pottery dinner service made by The Old Hall Earthenware Company, about 1870. This design was also made full-size

This type of dolls' house furniture is commonly called 'Dolls' Duncan Phyfe' and dates from the mid-nineteenth century. Several pieces are marked with their original price, ranging from 3d to 1/6d

Dolls' House Furniture

Few dolls' houses contain furniture of one period, new pieces having been added with each generation of children, and it would be unwise to date any house by its contents, which are usually more intriguing than the house itself.

Many of the small tin utensils found in the kitchens are similar to those in the larger model rooms known as *Nuremberg Kitchens*, though those intended for a dolls' house are usually smaller, and less detailed. The kitchens evoke the period with their Dutch ovens, bottle-jacks, skimmers and large saws for cutting up meat. Cheap white-wood Bavarian furniture is often used to furnish the kitchen and is sometimes given blue or red decoration. Kitchen ranges are sometimes fine miniature models and at other times mere suggestions.

The greatest pains were taken over the furnishing of the drawing-rooms, in order to create an atmosphere of opulence. Beaded footstools, tiny embroidered antimacassars, small

German metal picture frames, and fire-places with splendidly swirling flames are found. Papier-mâché, tin, cane and paper, as well as wood, were used in the making of small furniture. The most attractive is that traditionally known among collectors as 'Dolls' Duncan Phyfe' which, though bearing little resemblance to the furniture of the famous American maker, is a useful term to cover the group of furniture made of imitation rosewood and decorated with gilt transfer-work. It is often seen in good-quality Victorian dolls' houses and is an excellent foil for the Parian busts of royalty, glass vases, writing-stands and imitation brass and pewter trays, that crowd such interiors.

Fretwork became very popular as a hobby at the end of the century and home-made furniture of this type is to be found alongside such commercially made examples as the bentwood furniture illustrated.

A set of dolls' house furniture made of cane in imitation of the bentwood furniture so popular from the 1870s. Reputed to have belonged to the family of the Duke of Devonshire. About 1880

Dolls' Houses of the Nineteenth and the Twentieth Centuries
The Nineteenth Century

Though many nineteenth-century dolls' houses exhibit fine workmanship, they are no longer the exquisitely made drawing-room toys of the seventeenth and eighteenth centuries. They have become entirely children's toys and only rarely have locks or carrying-handles and, though the furnishings in estate-made houses might still be craftsman-made, they are more usually mass-produced and bought from toyshops.

The dolls' house had now become basically a box with simple partitions, quite often even the staircase being omitted. Queen Victoria owned a very basic house of this type, which has only one room on either floor and is very sparsely furnished.

Dutch dolls' houses of the period often look misleadingly old, as they were made in traditional designs, the French houses, in contrast, having a charming, frivolous appeal and being very light to handle, though made of wood. German houses were made commercially at Augsburg, Ulm and Hesse-Kassel, where fine shops and cafés were also manufactured.

The exterior of a beautiful dolls' house of about 1880 from the Penshurst Place Toy Museum in Kent

A room from a mid-nineteenth century house which is interesting as it is constructed in a cabinet in the eighteenth-century idiom. The interior shows some good furniture, especially the mirror

The Museum of the City of New York has good examples of dolls' houses made in the United States, which are similar to the English in style, though the American makers appear to have been fond of using a coating of sand over glue to give a stone-like effect, which was never as popular in England. One interesting American house is that built by L. V. Badger in 1818, being a replica of his old family home, which had been built in 1690. The house, though accurate in detail, was intended as a toy for his children, and Mr Badger made most of the furniture himself. This type of retrospective model was unusual in the nineteenth century, when up-to-date designs were preferred.

The detail on the facades of many of these dolls' houses, with their splendid porches and fine large bay windows, is usually well planned, as are many of the effective wood and metal fireplaces, which were built into the original structure. Doors were often made permanently closed and often have the

French house, about 1870, with storage space in the roof for furniture. The bisque boy doll standing in the parlour is attractive. Wall and floor papers are original, except in parlour

metal lion's mask door-knocker in imitation brass, seen on dolls' houses from most countries.

One of the advances of the nineteenth century was the production of papers especially for dolls' houses, floor papers being made to represent carpet, linoleum and parquet. Wallpapers suitable for simple kitchens, or drawing-rooms of the most elegant *décor*, were all available.

Cardboard houses were produced with brightly coloured printed fronts, and others were produced from sheets of paper to be pasted on board at home, and then assembled. These small houses are usually badly damaged and are also difficult to furnish, as the scale is so small.

Cheap board and wood houses that were about 14 ins. (35 cm.) high were made in the eighteenth century, and were of poor finish and quality, which probably accounts for their failure to survive, though they can be seen in old prints of toyshops. The eighteenth-century houses, with which we are familiar, are those especially made for very wealthy families. It is therefore not true to say that the standard of dolls' houses was in decline in the nineteenth century, rather that attractive, strong houses became available to middle-class children. The general standard, in fact, probably improved, as the houses could be made in a far greater range, and by 1896 Morrell's were offering dolls' houses from '3/6d. to £10.10s.' at their Oxford Street shop. Dolls and the range of furnishings generally available improved steadily during the century, reaching their peak around 1900.

Most of the eighteenth-century dolls' houses had contents added during the Victorian period, which give the interiors their great charm and except when such a standard as that exhibited in the Uppark Baby House is set, many would probably be very cold and austere in their original state.

The Twentieth Century

The interest in dolls' houses exhibited by Queen Mary, who so enriched the collections of several London museums with

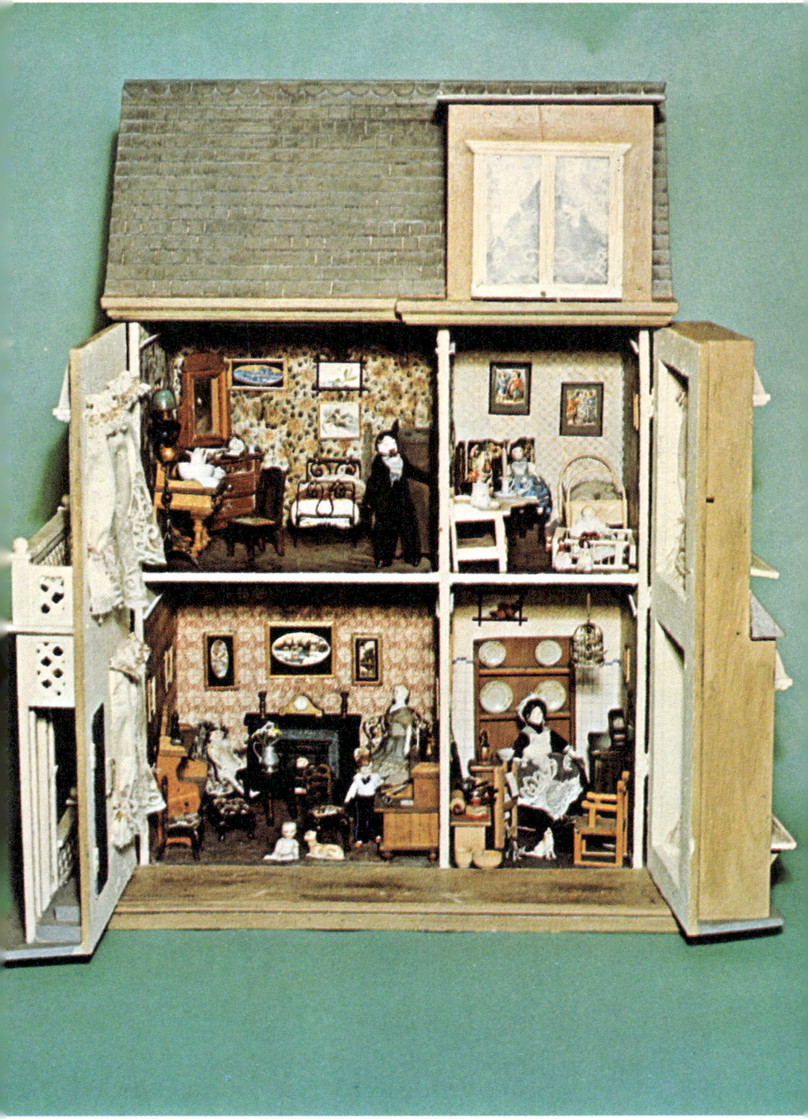

Queen Mary's Dolls' House. The Queen's bedroom has a painting of the Duchess of Teck by Frank Salisbury, a ceiling by Glyn Philpot and a carpet made by the Stratford-on-Avon School of Needlework

the nineteenth-century houses she had refurnished, encouraged many others to follow her example. Realizing how poorly the mass-produced toys of the twentieth century compared with those of previous generations, many adults once again took an interest in what had essentially been a child's toy during the previous century. They amused themselves by the skilful furnishing of models often made at home. Fantastic heights of extravagance were reached, such as is seen in Sir Neville Wilkinson's *Titania's Palace*, or Queen Mary's Dolls' House, which was designed by Sir Edwin Lutyens in 1924, and furnished by the best available craftsmen and manufacturers.

Other people, collecting within their price range, created houses simply for the fun of making the furnishings themselves. One house of this period has been most painstakingly decorated in Edwardian style and peopled with Victorian dolls. The furniture has been skilfully made from embossed cartons of the period and decorated with card moulding. Bed covers and carpets, carefully worked, must have taken several years to complete.

Old furniture has often been added to such houses, sometimes giving them a deceptively antique appearance. In fact, most of the houses made in this period tend to be retrospective in character, and directed towards the taste of adults. Some of the English newspapers, inspired by Queen Mary's Dolls' House, also constructed houses for exhibition purposes, but these are now mainly known from contemporary illustrations.

A few houses made in the early years of this century do reflect current designs, such as the dolls' house in the Bethnal Green Museum given by Miss Pollock and the one given by the Hon Mrs Thorold. The latter house, in the style of the 1920s is particularly interesting, though it desperately needs some dolls of the period to make it complete.

The library equals the opulence of the bedroom. The ceiling is by William Walcot. Cabinets with large drawers contain seven hundred works by contemporary artists. Books are written in by authors like J. M. Barrie and G. K. Chesterton

Dolls' wrought-iron bed, 24 ins. (61 cm.), with optional canopy. Probably French, 1880. Similar cradles were also made. Simon & Halbig doll

Cots, Beds and Cradles

Edwardian postcards show the wide variety of dolls' beds which were available during the period. Many beds were made of cast and wrought iron, which could create a very light and pretty effect, while at the same time being strong enough to stand a great deal of wear, as is evidenced by the number that have survived. Swinging cradles, cots with brass knobs, and beds with canopies, were all made of iron, often decorated with touches of colour on the ground colour, which was usually white. Though often badly rusted, these toys can be rubbed down with a wire brush, treated with a metal primer, and then painted to something like their original state.

Wood has remained the favourite material, and cradles in particular were often made at home. The larger of the two illustrated cradles was made by a carpenter for his daughter, especially to fit a wax doll. The smaller cradle was commercially produced, and bought originally in a Scottish toyshop at the end of the last century. The variety of shapes in which babies' cradles were made during the century is reflected in the miniature versions, some of which were made in great detail, being finely panelled and carved in fruit wood, mahogany or pine. Though cradles were made in miniature from the Middle Ages, most available examples are nineteenth-century. Fine joints and exceptional attention to detail are sometimes an indication of an early date.

Particularly splendid half tester beds were made of mahogany, and given well-made hangings and buttoned mattresses. Many of these half testers fall into the category of fine miniature furniture rather than toys, and the excellent state of repair which is usual is an indication that they were played with as best toys, probably under supervision. Though fake antique toy cradles are sometimes found, it is most unusual to find a faked half tester, as there is too much detailed work involved for it to be commercially viable.

Two cradles, about 1870. The smaller was commercially made in Scotland, while the carved cradle was made by a Welsh cabinet-maker

The 'Schoenhut Humpty Dumpty Circus', 1903. Made in America by a German *émigré*. The designer was anonymous and insisted on selling the invention for one hundred dollars. A few examples from the many available

Acrobatic Toys

The Pantin, which so amused the ladies of the French court, appeared in the mid-eighteenth century and has enjoyed continuous popularity, as it could easily adapt to current fashion and was cheap to produce in paper or board. It is sometimes seen in more sophisticated form, made of finely carved bone, ivory or wood, but such versions of the Jumping Jack were usually intended to amuse adults. Various sizes were made, the Museum of Childhood in Edinburgh having one that is 4 ft. (1·2 m.) tall!

The Acrobats which Crandall made in America in 1874 (see title page) are similar inexpensive toys, though the figures are cut from board ½ in. (1·4 cm.) thick, and have dowel-turned limbs ending in blocks of wood for hands and feet which could be slotted together enabling the group to balance in a variety of poses.

Acrobatic toys in particular were made in America, and it

is from the United States that the 'Humpty-Dumpty Circus' originated in 1903. The circus was made by A. Schoenhut of Philadelphia and included something like one hundred characters which could be bought separately. All the figures and animals are well articulated and can assume almost any natural pose, so that a clown can balance on one leg or stand upside down on a ladder supported by a groove cut in his hand.

Motive power was also supplied by the torque principle, as with the 'monkey on a stick', and pneumatic power was employed in toys such as a pair of India Rubber Prize Fighters, actuated separately by pressure on the controlling rubber bulbs. This toy cost 10/6d. when it was made in 1896.

Many variations of the balance principle are to be found, though many of the more scientific toys are fascinating but rather unattractive.

Weighted tumbling acrobats, probably of German origin. Toys of this type were activated by mercury or a system of threads and weights

An animated musical Christmas party. German, late nineteenth century. Musical boxes of this type occasionally appear on the market but are expensive to buy (about £250)

Musical Toys

Simple musical boxes with a winder on the top, and a picture, perhaps of children playing, or a nursery rhyme, can still be bought for a few pounds, though the more complicated musical toys have really become too expensive for most new collectors. Toy gramophones are interesting, as juvenile records can be searched for, the illustrated gramophone having been bought with a recording of 'Chick, chick, chick, chick, chicken'.

In buying any musical toy, condition is all-important, as it is difficult to find a repairer, so, unless mechanically minded, it is advisable to avoid anything that does not work, as the odds are that it never will.

Poupards, the dolls mounted on sticks, which play a tune when swung around, are attractive, being made by both French and German makers, and have the variety of heads found on dolls from both countries. Their rich costume, decorated with ribbons, makes them attractive as well as interesting. The French dollmakers often put automated dolls on musical boxes, perhaps a boy playing an instrument which moves as the music plays, or even a group of musicians such as that made by Jacquet Droz, where one figure plays a drum, another a fiddle and an old lady performs on an accordion.

The polyphon, which was controlled by a metal disc with slots cut corresponding to notes, is sometimes found in versions made especially for children, though usually the distinguishing factor is simply the method of decoration, the children's versions being decorated perhaps with fairies or toys.

Johann Nepomuk Mälzel is said to have introduced the first method of reproducing speech. The method was by a bellows action, pumped alternately by the right and left arms and sending sound through a reed to a voice-box. The valve made an explosive double sound 'Pa-Pa', then, muffled by another apparatus, the sound was repeated as 'Ma-Ma'.

Toy gramophone made around 1920 which still plays. A large variety of records for the juvenile market were available

An automaton of a woman playing the piano. When the string is pulled the woman appears to be playing the piano to the accompaniment of music

Automata in the Nineteenth Century

The fine craftsman-made 'princes' toys, such as those made in the eighteenth century by Jacques de Vaucanson, the silversmith, Du Moulin, and the Family of Jacquet Droz, have disappeared, and those of nineteenth-century origin exhibit an appeal which was aimed at the child, though such toys were expensive until clockwork mechanisms began to be mass-produced.

In the *Girls' Own Book* of 1848 is a description of automata: 'There was a chess player, an image dressed like a Turk; who sat at the board and played as good a game of chess as if he had brains in his wooden skull. He shook his head and rapped the board with his fingers when his adversary made a move contrary to the rules of the game, and when he had the king in his power he called "Echec."'. Another automaton was a roundabout, which had a number of circus figures riding around and performing feats which called for extreme mechanical skill. A Spanish lancer caught a little cap on the point of his lance without stopping his horse, which was apparently made of wood with jointed legs. A slow clumsy clown was chased by a horse, which overtook him and snatched his hat from his head, while Harlequin on his own very troublesome horse attempted to help his friend! This almost unbelievable toy is said to have been made by Johann Mälzel, who also invented the speech mechanism previously mentioned.

Many 'walking' dolls actually moved on a wheeled base hidden by a long skirt. One doll is described in 1815 which walked by placing one foot before the other, while turning its head. The most famous walking doll is that articulated by a spring and known as the *Autoperipatetikos*, which was invented by Enoch Rise Morrison of New York, though most of the clockwork mechanisms found on automated dolls of the late nineteenth century were made at the workshops of Roullet & Decamps in Paris.

A rather sophisticated automaton which would have appealed more to adults than to children, of a ship tossed by waves

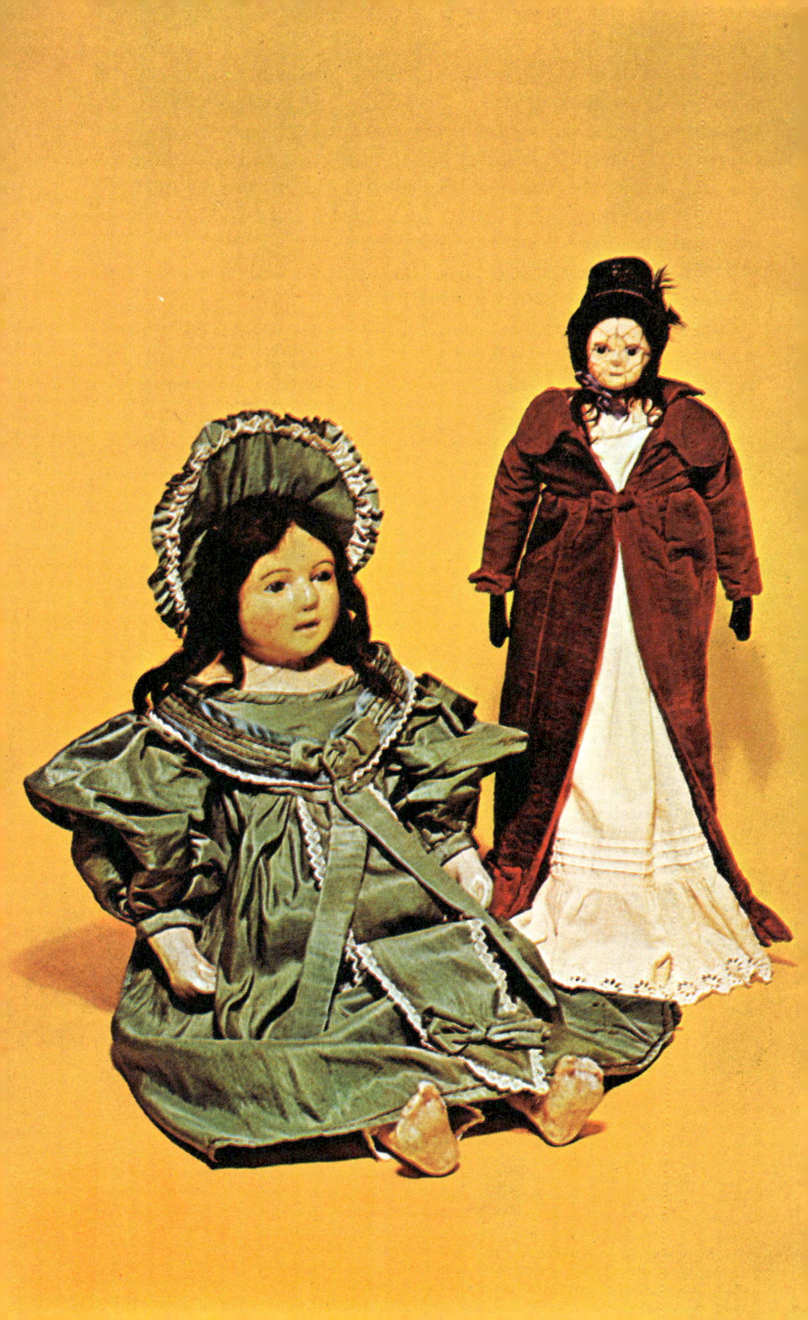

Wax Dolls
The Nineteenth Century

In a water-colour, dated 1836, illustrating a bedroom, is a wax doll about 3 ft. (92 cm.) tall and fashionably dressed. The room is that of a wealthy lady, the doll being obviously a decorative item in a room which bears no other evidence of a child. One wonders how many of the dolls, which we think were looked after so carefully by children, were in fact purely decorative frivolities.

The above-mentioned doll is one of a type ghoulishly referred to by collectors as 'slit heads' because of the method of inserting the wig through a cut in the composition substance of the head. When new, these dolls would have looked quite attractive, but the differing rate of contraction between the wax with which the head was coated and the composition, has normally caused severe cracking, and the dolls have usually assumed a macabre appearance, which accounts for the fact that, despite their age, they command low prices.

Composition dolls were made in the seventeenth century, and solid wax heads were common in the eighteenth, but the dipping of the composition cast into a bath of wax, to give a more lifelike effect, was used particularly in the nineteenth century. Pupil-less glass eyes were inserted into the eye sockets, and eyebrows and lips painted on, to give greater realism.

The body is usually a series of rectangular sawdust-filled bags with coloured leather forearms often added, perhaps to give the effect of gloves. Only three fingers were indicated to make the hands appear narrow.

Sleeping eye mechanisms are sometimes found on similar dolls, and occasionally a simple voice-box worked by string. The type of doll described was often referred to as a 'Bagman's Baby', as it was sold cheaply by pedlars.

An odious practice has sprung up, actually commended by some collectors, of re-dipping dolls of this type to improve their complexions, but as they are ruined as antiques, it is only forgivable if almost all the wax has flaked away.

The standing doll with black pupil-less eyes is the type known as a 'slit-head' and was made about 1830. The seated doll has a full-domed head. Hands and feet more realistic than usual, c. 1840

Pumpkin head, about 1860. The original wooden arms with separated fingers are unusual in this type. Straw-stuffed body with a squeaker. Known as 'Granny Sidebotham's doll' by family which once owned it

Later Developments

Waxed composition dolls, whose hair is moulded in one with the face, are often referred to as 'squash heads' or 'pumpkin heads' due to the roundness of the face and the narrow width from front to back. Large, black, pupil-less eyes are again common in this type of doll, which was popular in the middle of the nineteenth century. These dolls usually have wooden lower arms and legs, with painted details. A squeaker voice-box is also fairly common. Unusual examples have intricate hair-styles, with combs and bows, and sometimes a hat or bonnet moulded in one with the hair. Though these dolls have an attractive primitive charm, they are not as sought-after as many of the later bisques.

By the end of the nineteenth century there was a variety of waxed composition dolls, some of which were made with great realism, while others were tawdry in the extreme, sometimes having bodies roughly filled with straw. Composition limbs were often painted to represent boots in the current fashion, and teeth are occasionally found behind slightly parted lips. Pierced ears sometimes carry ear-rings, which are often hidden by the thick mohair wigs.

A method of making a wax mould and pouring plaster into it became popular at the end of the century, but dolls made by this method are extremely difficult to repair, as the inner shell has often broken away, especially if, as in some late versions, the sleeping eyes are worked by a lead counter-weight mechanism.

The illustrated doll in pink is interesting, as the boots are orange and gold, rather than the usual black, and were wax-dipped to give a good finish. This doll once belonged to a Yorkshire family and came into my collection still wrapped in the Paisley shawl in which the owner had once carried it.

Two waxed composition dolls with attached wigs, made about 1870. The seated doll is unusual because of the orange and gold waxed boots. Plain black boots are more usual

Wooden Dolls

Vast quantities of simple wooden jointed dolls were made during the nineteenth century in Sonneberg, Oberammergau and the Grödner Tal. The most common wooden dolls are popularly known as 'wooden tops'. Care should be taken in buying such dolls, as they are still made today, and many modern examples, dressed as pedlar dolls, can be found in antique shops. An indication of old Dutch dolls are the carved spade-like hands and rather heavy wood. The modern versions are featherlight.

A rather more delicate version of the 'wooden top' is that usually referred to as a 'Grödner Tal' which is the type of 'Penny Wooden' dressed by Queen Victoria and her governess. These dolls have well articulated bodies, and are characterized by upswept black hair held in place with an orange or yellow comb. Many of these small dolls can still be seen in dolls' houses, but the larger versions are much rarer.

A 'Grödner Tal' doll, probably made for a dolls' house. This is the type of doll dressed by Queen Victoria as a child. The yellow comb is often found on dolls of this type. Joints still move easily

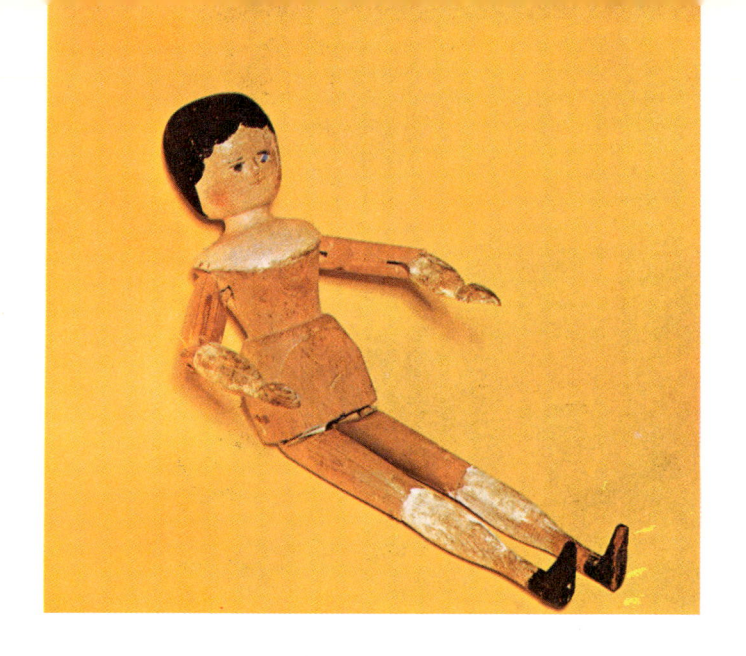

Big 'wooden top', about 1850. The large spade-like hands are a feature of the older dolls of this type. Late examples have stick-like hands and feet

The Smithsonian Institution in Washington D.C. has a fine ball-jointed doll circa 1810, which wears a gold tiara and has flowers painted on the chest section. This very large doll could have been used as a dressmaker's model, as it is also jointed at the waist. Most of the makers of wooden dolls included lay figures among their products.

The Ellis wooden doll is justly famous in America. The patent for this doll was registered in 1873 and was for a doll of rock maple with mortise and tennon joints, and pewter or iron hands and feet, the head being shaped under hydraulic pressure. The feet of the Ellis doll were always jointed so that various positions could be assumed. Good American dolls were also made by Mason and Taylor, who made a variety of models, even a few black dolls. Some of their products had metal hands and feet, and others had turning heads.

A porcelain lustre doll, about 1850, with original coral necklace and clothes. Probably made in Germany. 21 ins. (53 cm.) high

Porcelain Dolls

The porcelain doll, more than any other, is the true Victorian. Palefaced and primly coiffured, it is the woman that gazes superciliously at us from fashion prints. The hairstyle is probably the best means of dating such dolls, though even this is not altogether reliable, as fashion in dolls tends to be rather retrospective.

Porcelain dolls were particularly popular during the middle of the nineteenth century and, even though they were being referred to as old-fashioned in the 1870s, they continued to be made for many years. Henry Mayhew, the nineteenth-century writer, comments that the principal source of such heads was Hamburg, and that they were sold in London at Alfred Davis's, and White's in Houndsditch, and Joseph's in Leadenhall Street. The hawkers of such dolls apparently assembled them at home and sold them from baskets.

What could be described as a porcelain doll in its most ordinary form would be a shoulder head with short black hair and blue eyes, the porcelain legs ending in black boots. The illustrated dolls' house dolls fall quite neatly into this category, but the large doll has an attractive pink lustre glaze, which makes it rather more desirable.

As most porcelain heads are unmarked except for numerals, they are almost impossible to attribute, though obviously the majority were made in Germany. Jacob Petit in Fontainebleau attempted to break the German monopoly and produced some good heads which are marked, and characterized by eight holes, instead of the usual four allowed for sewing the head to the body.

Rare porcelains are characterized by unusual hairstyles, set-in glass eyes, pierced ears, and heads made without hair to which a mohair wig could be attached. A few very good porcelains have teeth, though this is very unusual. A porcelain with blonde hair or brown eyes is also a good acquisition for a collection.

A group of the more common type of porcelain dolls with white faces and black hair. This type of doll was made into the 1920s. The doll in the Edwardian bath is known as a 'Frozen Charlotte'

A fine, large papier-mâché head with unusual hair-style, 1830s. Often called a milliner's model. Hair drawn back into a bun is more usual

Papier-Mâché and Composition Dolls

The attractive golden colour which the papier mâché dolls that were made between 1820 and 1850 have developed, often gives them an appearance of great antiquity. The well moulded, lightly varnished heads were made in France and Germany and attached to slim, tall, leather bodies. Arms and legs were usually made of wood, the join between the wood and leather being neatened by a strip of coloured paper. Completely undamaged shoulder heads are rare, as most of them have cracked due to storage in an unfavourable atmosphere. Dolls of this type are made more interesting by the extravagance of their hairstyles, the plainer *coiffures* being less desirable to a collector.

I have never seen a papier-mâché of this period with fair hair, but examples with set-in glass eyes are recorded, so perhaps a blonde papier-mâché will one day appear. Though dolls of this type were usually intended as playthings, the weight of one example, 34 ins. (86 cm.) tall, which I bought recently, made me wonder if this was always the case, as the doll was far too heavy for a child to carry.

After 1850 many different methods of making good composition substances were attempted, the Greiner dolls, patented in America in 1858, being the first American manufactured dolls. The cloth, which the firm used to reinforce the pressed paper, now often shows through in a disfiguring way. Most of the dolls produced around the middle of the century, both in Europe and America, resemble the black-haired porcelain dolls, though their average size is larger.

Composition dolls, with painted or glass eyes, made to resemble children, were very common by the Edwardian period, sometimes with the same heads as are found waxed, the composition version being even less expensive. Dolls of this type have stuffed cloth bodies with composition arms and legs, usually with black boots on the feet. Fashionable lady dolls of this substance were made around 1900, which creates an interesting throw-back to the lady dolls of the Regency period.

Composition baby doll with attractive dimpled face and fixed glass eyes, about 1880. Good original clothes with great detail

Parian Dolls

The parian substance, whose invention was so disputed, was in general use by 1850, and dollmakers were quick to take advantage of the fine modelling that could be achieved in the new material. Parian combines a fine surface with a dense body, and dolls' heads made of parian withstood knocks much better than heads made of thin porcelain. Due to the strength of the substance, the modeller attempted heights of extravagance which have never been surpassed in dollmaking. Extremely elaborate hairstyles were arranged with ribbons, flowers, beads and combs, giving elegant detail on the skilfully modelled hair.

The finest parian heads have chalk-white faces relieved by very delicate tinting. Black or brown hair is unusual, as blonde hair was better suited to this medium, which took delicate colouring more successfully. A few rare parian dolls have swivel heads, while others have set-in eyes, pierced ears, or necklaces moulded on the shoulder-plate.

French Parian doll 1860–70. Under the dress is a red and white striped crinoline. Flat-heeled black boots. Cloth body

Parian doll with lustre and enamel turban of the type worn for evening in the 1850s. Hair of a red tone. Flat boots with ribbons

Many of these heads cost very little, and some were used on the tops of pin cushions and tea cosies, which accounts for the large number of heads that have survived without bodies. The doll, if complete, should have arms and legs also made of parian, the feet often ending in coloured boots, rather like those worn by the porcelain dolls.

Dating these dolls, which were made both in France and Germany, is helped by the type of shoes worn, as those with heels usually date from after 1870. The method of dressing the hair is also of some help, but too much reliance should not be placed on either of these factors, as the original moulds were used for many years.

Many parian dolls have been given names such as 'Mary Todd Lincoln', 'Amelia Bloomer', or 'the Empress Eugénie', but these names should be treated in the same way as most of the pretty stories in the world of antiques.

Blonde Bisque Dolls

Many early bisque dolls closely resemble the porcelain dolls, both in the construction of the body and the shape of the head, but the soft, textured effect of the bisque makes them much more realistic. These dolls lack the cool aloofness of the parian dolls and are rather lighter to handle. There is much more the look of a toy about bisque dolls, whereas the parians look as though they would be happiest sitting on a dressing-table.

Boy dolls with short curled hair became more popular at the end of the century, though some of the lady dolls made at that period, when short hairstyles were fashionable, can be mistaken for boy dolls. An interesting German boy doll in my collection has his complete shirt moulded in one with the head, the shirt being tied at the neck with a large, nicely modelled bow.

Most of the bisque dolls were made in Germany and very few are marked, though I have seen two with the Simon and Halbig mark. Dolls' heads of this type were imported into France to be used on early Jumeau dolls. Many blonde bisques had necklaces moulded on the neckline, while some late examples have a name, such as 'Ethel', written on the shoulder.

Although most blonde bisque dolls are mounted on cotton bodies, some were given bodies and arms of leather, while others had bisque forearms.

Many 'bonnet' dolls were made of bisque, and as these are usually fairly small, they can form an interesting group, though some of the late German and Japanese 'bonnet' dolls with fixed limbs are tawdry in the extreme. The bisque dolls' house dolls are probably the best dolls' house inhabitants ever produced; the boy doll, illustrated in the house on page 81 being a good example, as is the blonde bisque lady doll that sits on a sofa.

A group of dolls often referred to as blonde bisques to differentiate them from the later bisque dolls. The lady doll with short hair dates from the 1880s, when short hair again became fashionable. The turned head is unusual as is the leather body. A stuffed cloth body is more usual on this type of doll. The Scottish dressed boy doll is a nice acquisition, as boy dolls are harder to find

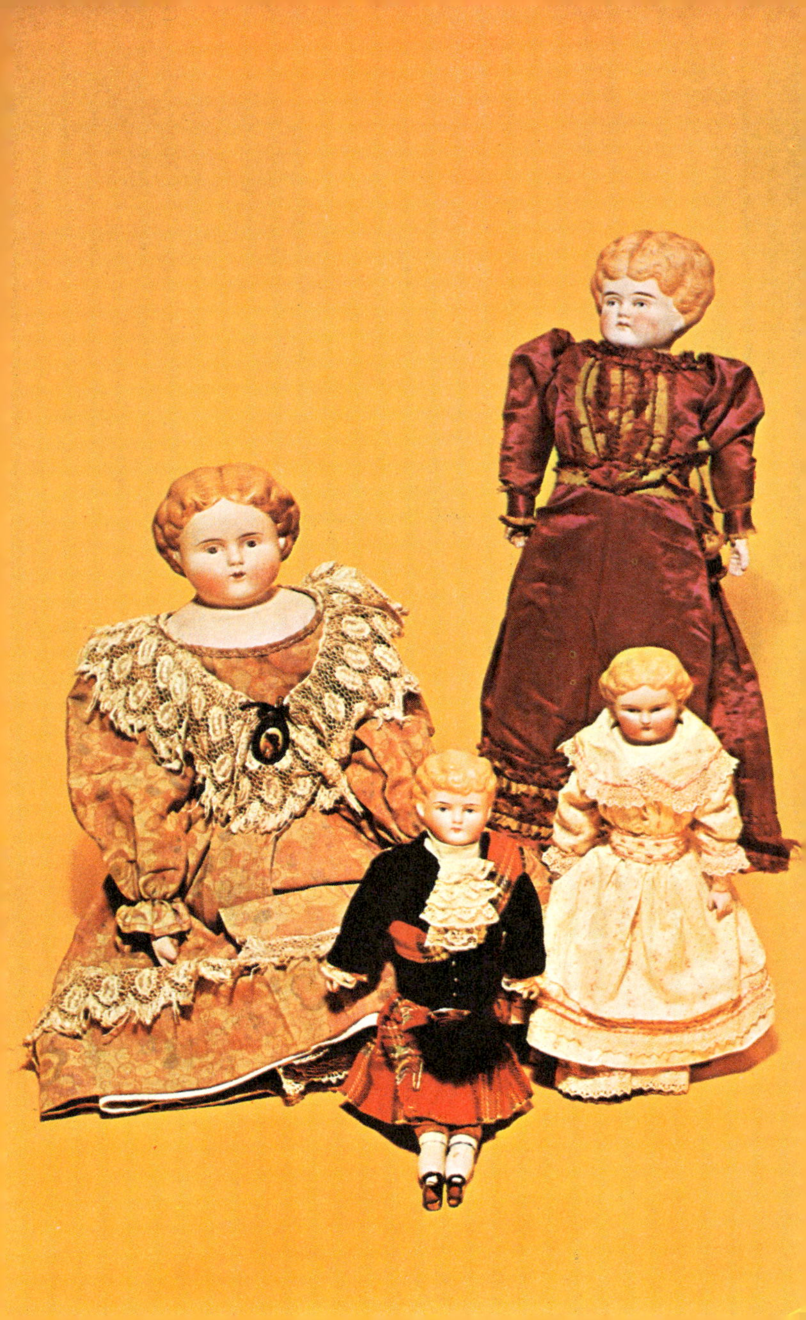

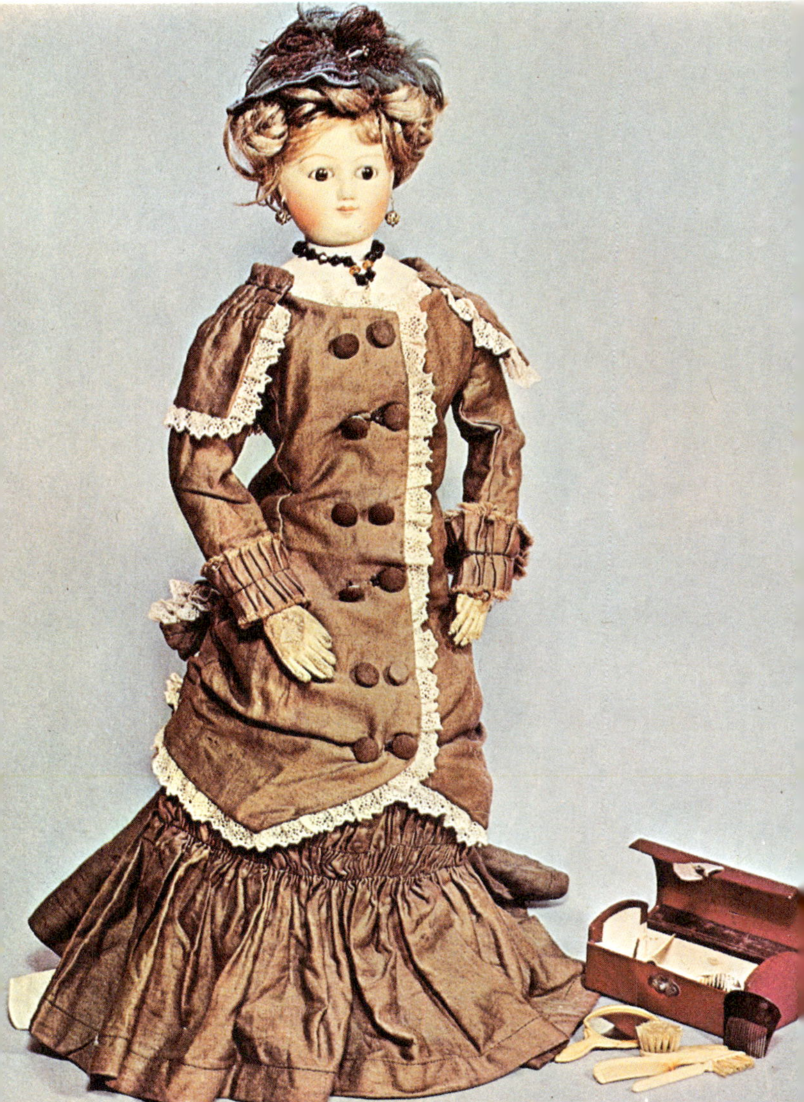

Fashion Dolls or *Parisiennes*

Early fashion dolls were sometimes fully life-sized and used for sending copies of current designs from country to country. They were used a great deal before fashion magazines made them redundant, though they have been used occasionally, even to the present day, to show off a dress or a design.

The French lady dolls made between 1860 and 1890 became known as Fashion Dolls, as they were so often dressed in fine Parisian costume. The term, however, has little meaning, as it covers a wide range of dolls which were intended as playthings, admittedly on rather an expensive scale.

Bodies of wood and composition are found on *Parisiennes*, besides the gussetted leather bodies, that are most common. The leather bodies are very finely made, with very small inserted gussets and carefully stitched separated fingers. Swivel necks are usually a feature of such dolls, but there are exceptions with fixed heads. A cork *pate*, fixed to the top of the head, gave a good surface for the fixing of an intricate hairstyle in position.

Many of these bisque shoulder-headed dolls are unmarked and have to be attributed by resemblance to known products of firms such as Bru, Simonne, Jumeau, and Cremer.

The *Parisienne* was often accompanied by a trunk, which held a lavish supply of clothes, hats and dressing equipment, though it is difficult to find a doll that has retained all its belongings. The clothes were usually well-made and have an eye-catching appeal because of their elegance.

As *Parisiennes* often command high prices, they have been reproduced in great numbers. Suspicion should be aroused by any doll whose body is in good condition, but which has no clothing, and by a bisque of a texture that is either very granular, or over-smooth and highly coloured.

A French fashion doll, dated by the original clothes to the 1870s. Though the dress is well made, the underwear is very simply constructed, unlike home-dressed dolls of the period, whose underwear is often beautifully made. Gusseted leather body; swivel neck. Hair piled up on top to disguise its tatty state, which is better than rewigging a doll. Case contains brushes and toothcombs for fleas!

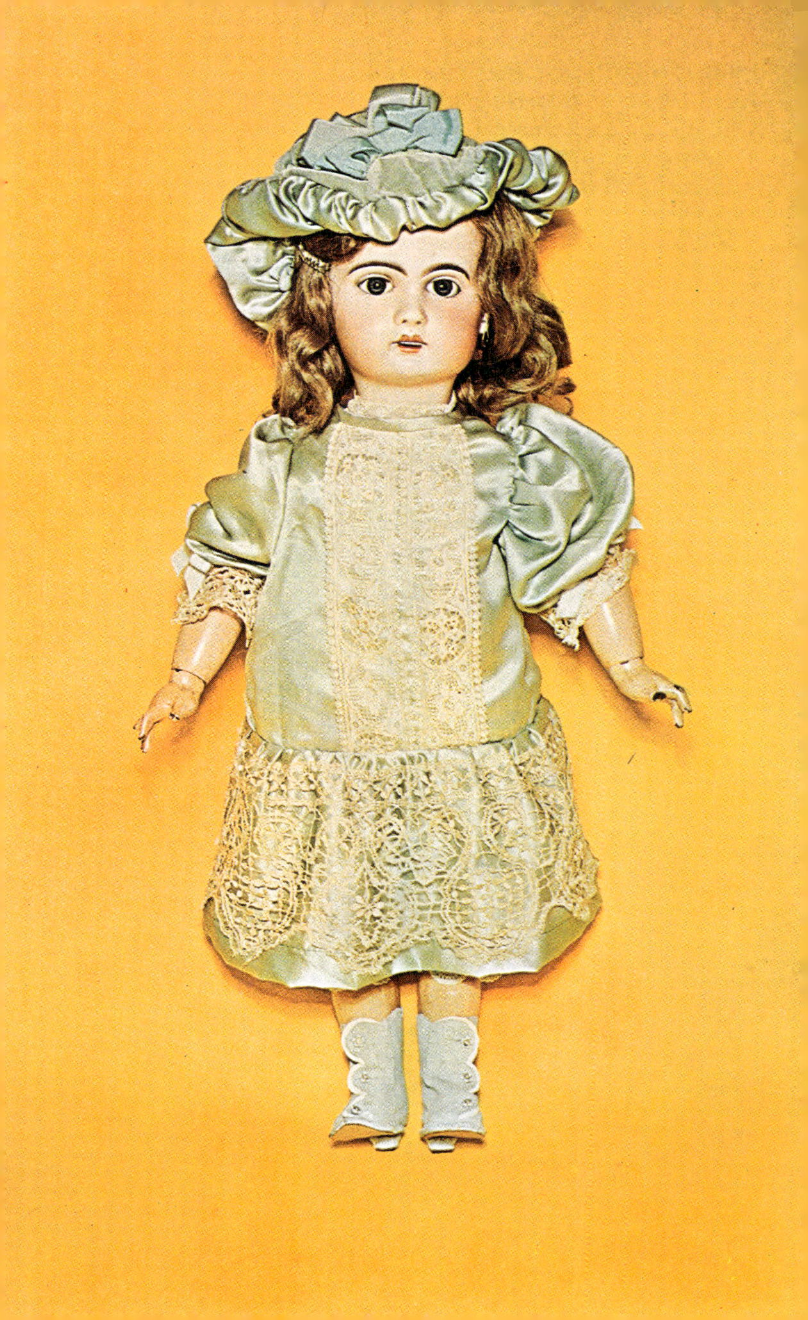

French Dolls
Jumeau

The Jumeau firm was well established by the middle of the nineteenth century, winning many medals at the exhibitions which were a feature of the period. The jury at the Great Exhibition of 1851, however, appears to have been more impressed by the clothes in which the dolls were dressed than by the dolls themselves, which they considered unexceptional, as the firm imported heads from Germany to use on their products. But by the end of the century, Jumeau heads were considered to be near perfection and gold medals were showered upon their products. Heads were now made by the Jumeau factory at Montreuil near Paris, and were characterized by their heavy features. The enormous eyes of early Jumeau dolls are also a peculiarity of the factory.

The bodies of the dolls were sometimes marked with the inscription '*Medaille d'Or 1878*', though this does not indicate the date of manufacture, merely the firm's pride in their achievement. Although the mark on the heads of some Jumeau dolls is incized, many were simply stamped on, or the dolls sometimes had a label attached to the body. Great care should be taken in purchasing, as unscrupulous dealers take advantage of the lack of incized marks. At a recent antiques fair a 'Jumeau' doll was for sale, which had been recently green-stamped over a faint incized German mark. At the same fair almost any unmarked doll was proudly labelled 'Jumeau'.

All the products of the firm are desirable acquisitions, but the long-faced, closed-mouth Jumeau is the most sought-after by collectors, though the dolls sold for musical boxes and automata are also fine investments. The Jumeau trade catalogues show the tremendous variety of costume in which the dolls could be supplied, many being on show at the firm's salesroom in the Rue Pastourelle in Paris, where they were exhibited in miniature settings.

A doll made from the Jumeau mould, probably after the amalgamation forming S.F.B.J. About 1905. The mechanism of this doll's body was patented in 1905. As it walks it lifts one hand towards the face simulating a blown kiss. The head turns and it cries: 'mama'. The large dark eyes are a feature of the better Jumeau dolls, as are the applied ears which are pierced.

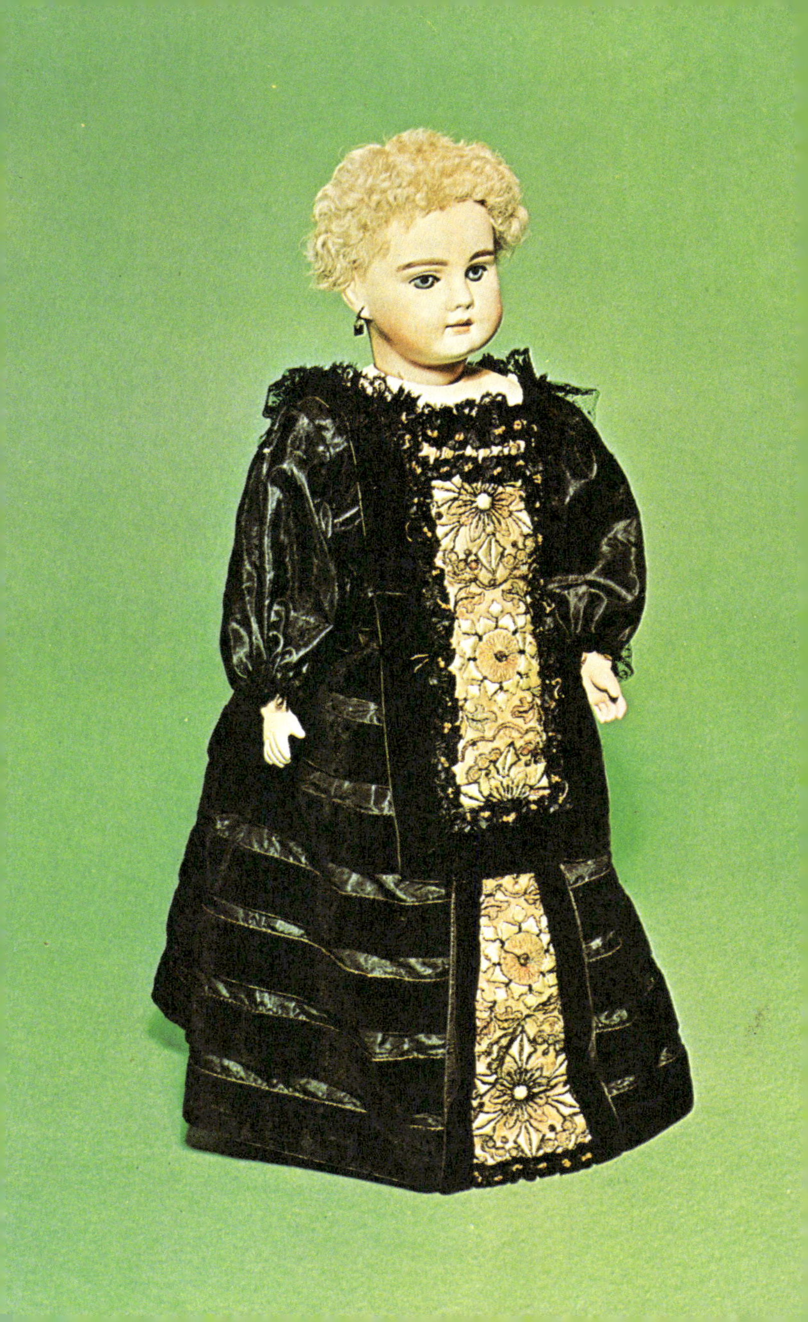

Bru

Dolls made by the firm of Bru are the most desirable of all to collectors, though they are not as commonly known as the products of the Jumeau factory. Bru marked their dolls with incized symbols, including a crescent shape, and a circle with a spot in the centre. The heads display more sensitivity than those of the Jumeau factory, and are of a deeper coloured bisque. The Bru kid-bodied dolls are characterized by their lightness, the illustrated doll having a cork-filled body on a wire armature. The cotton shape that formed the body was covered by a pink leather surface, whose construction compares favourably with the slimmer *Parisiennes*.

The Bru family were renowned for their innovations, from double-faced dolls to those that talked. *'Bébé Le Teteur'* sucked by itself, while another called *'Le Dormeur'* opened and closed its eyes naturally, by means of its eyelids. The most nauseating of all was a mama-and-papa doll that appeared to breathe. *'Bébé Petit Pas'* was a walking-and-talking *Bébé* with a winding mechanism, that must have been very irritating to a child who simply wanted a doll to nurse.

In 1883 the firm passed to H. Chevrot, and later to Eugène Girard, who both continued to produce dolls under the old name, and the number of innovations appears to have been undiminished.

Like the Jumeau firm, the company warned customers to buy only those dolls which carried the manufacturer's name, but as it was often stamped on the bodies, or simply on labels proudly carried, it has often disappeared and so we have to rely on the mark on the head or shoulders.

The company was as proud of their india-rubber dolls as it was of their composition dolls which were patented around 1890, though I have never actually seen an example of either of these types of doll.

Though this doll is dressed as a lady, it is of the type known as a *Bébé*, as the body is too plump to be a fashion doll, though the head swivels in the shoulder-plate, which is also bisque. Body of pink leather over a cloth lining. Cork-filled on a wire armature making a very light doll. Original lambskin wig. The slightly parted lips are often a feature of Bru dolls

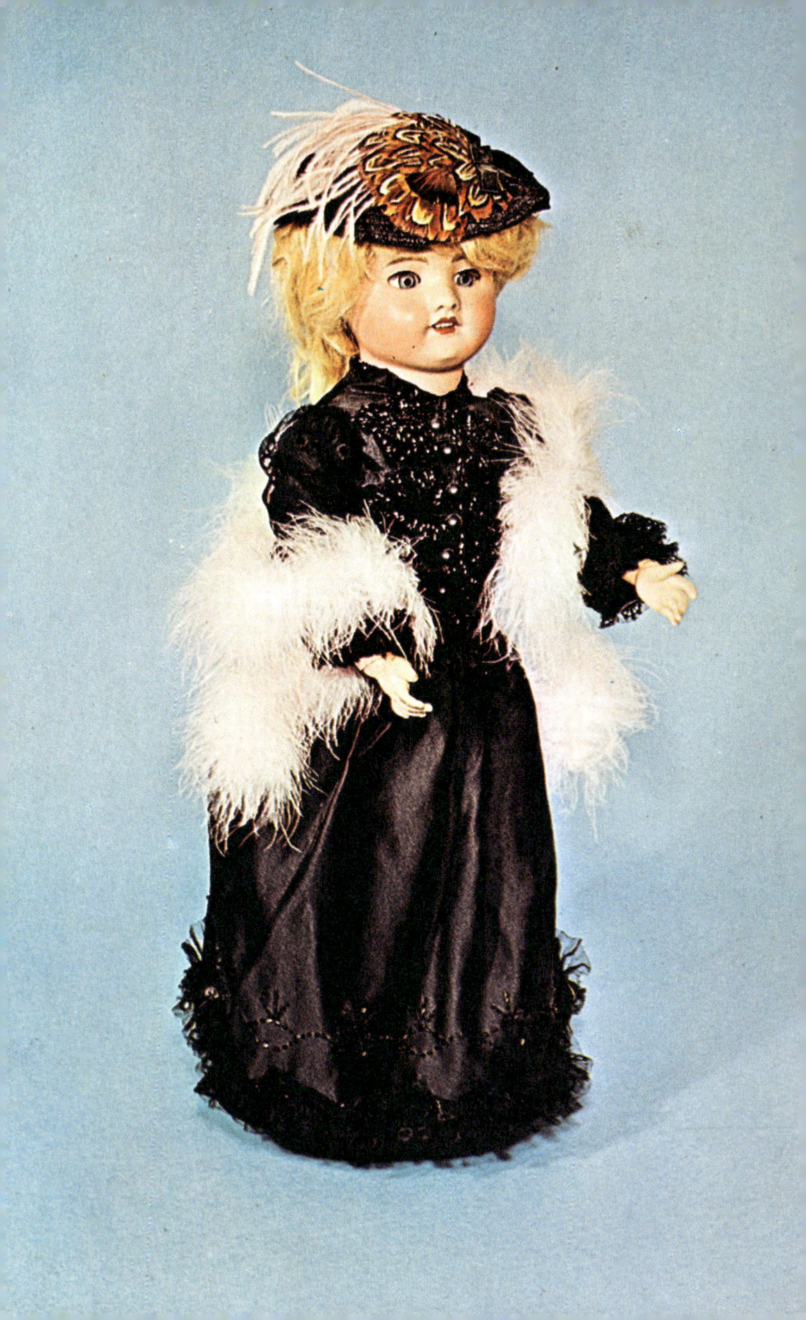

Société de Fabrication des Bébés et Jouets

German dollmakers had lagged behind the French in the production of attractive dolls. By the end of the nineteenth century, however, their mass-production methods had overtaken the French and, in an effort to cater for the ever-increasing mass-market, French firms grouped themselves together under the trade name of 'Société de Fabrication des Bébés et Jouets'. The group marked their products with the letters S.F.B.J., by which the firm is referred to by collectors. The rivalry which had long existed between firms such as Bru, Rabery & Delphieu, and Jumeau, appears to have been forgotten, and the group joined forces to combat the low-priced German dolls, which were flooding the European and American markets.

Moulds previously used by member companies were re-used, so that dolls bearing a strong resemblance to earlier Jumeau products are found marked S.F.B.J., while other heads look almost German in origin.

The S.F.B.J. doll illustrated is typical of the later products of the group, being well-made and with a very French-looking face, though not at all like the earlier Jumeaus.

S.F.B.J. produced dolls that walked, blew kisses or contained voice-boxes. Boy dolls were also made with attractively realistic faces, a good example being a particularly fine black doll. Coloured dolls had become much more popular, and attractive girl dolls were produced in both light and dark brown.

The Baby dolls have rather more character than is usually found, some having open-closed mouths and voice mechanisms. In 1912 the Vincennes factory was producing 5,000,000 dolls a year, a number that has ensured a good supply for the present-day collector, though obviously the dolls made from the Jumeau moulds are the most desirable.

A jointed doll made by S.F.B.J., about 1900. This is one of the more common types produced by the company. The jointing system on French dolls is better than that on German, and the anatomical detail rather more realistic. This doll was bought without clothes and a full-sized but very ragged lady's dress of the period was scaled down to fit the doll which is 24 ins. (61 cm.) high

Other French Makers

Fine dolls in the best French tradition were made by firms such as Schmitt, and Rabery & Delphieu. Steiner, in particular, made beautiful dolls, some with a highly complicated walking mechanism, while their coloured dolls are unsurpassed. Good Steiner dolls have become even more coveted than the products of the Jumeau factory and are increasingly difficult to find. French dolls, which are small or difficult to attribute, can still be bought fairly cheaply, however.

Schmitt made excellent quality dolls in the tradition of the fine *Bébés* and introduced an interesting, if somewhat impractical, technique, whereby a layer of wax was applied to the fired dolls' head in an attempt to further enhance the complexion. The dolls most commonly found in England are those made at Limoges, in particular the products of the Lanternier company, whose heads exhibit a wide variety of standard. The better heads are comparable with the best French makers, while the quality of the bisque in other versions is poor, and the tinting incredibly bad.

A variety of construction methods is found on French dolls, from those with metal-jointed parts, to bodies covered with stockinet or even made of gutta-percha. The dolls were often exquisitely dressed, some firms even running competitions for the submission of attractive new designs for dolls' clothes.

Roullet & Decamps made dolls with fascinating mechanisms, but usually used heads made by other firms, though a few exist marked with letters which could refer to the firm itself.

Rohmer dolls have very delicately shaped features, and the firm is interesting, as it introduced a method as early as 1858, by which a dolls' head could be turned by means of a cord running through the body.

It should be borne in mind that some French dolls are of poor quality and often cost less to buy than German examples.

French bisque dolls made between 1895 and 1910. The seated double-jointed doll in the fringed cape was made at the Lanternier factory in Limoges, as was the standing doll in pink. Limoges dolls are often of poor quality bisque, though others are acceptable. The seated doll in the sailor-dress was made by Paer Frères, about 1900

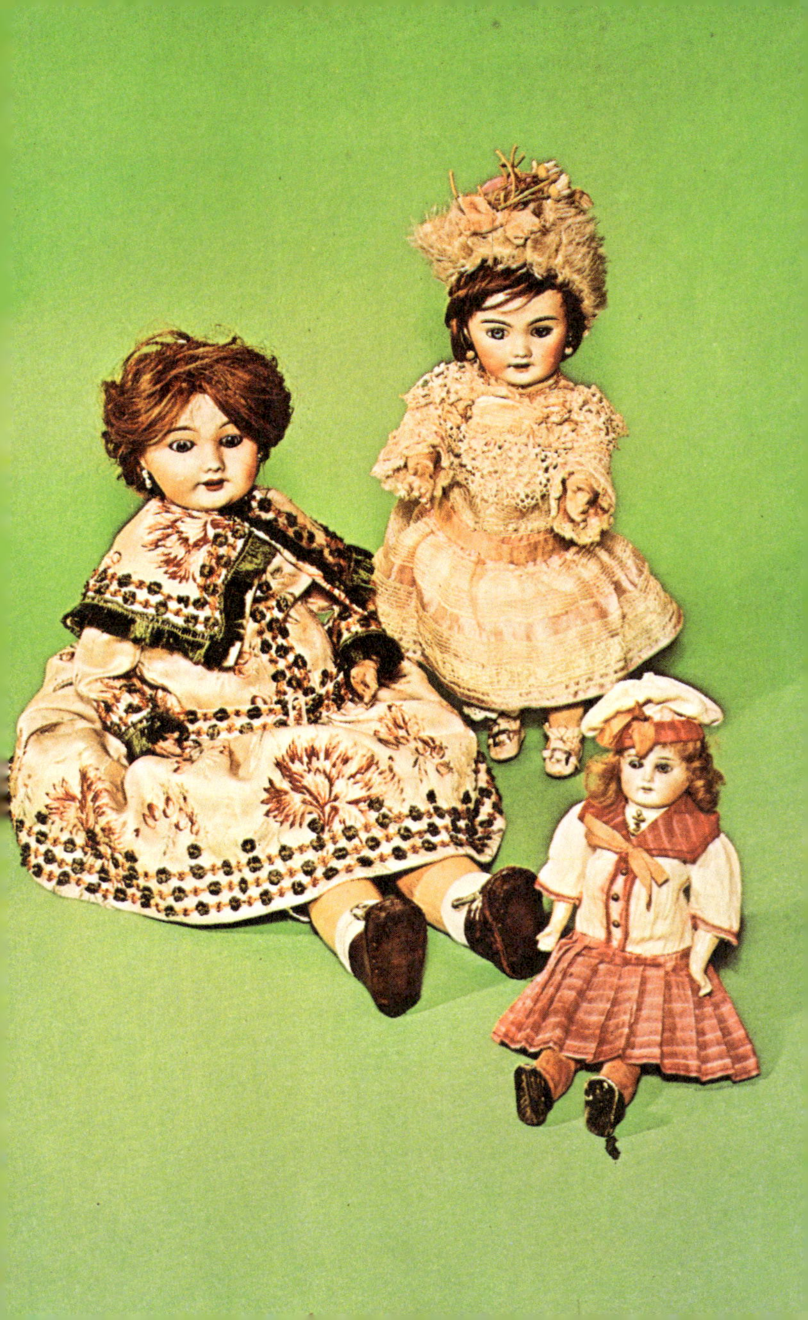

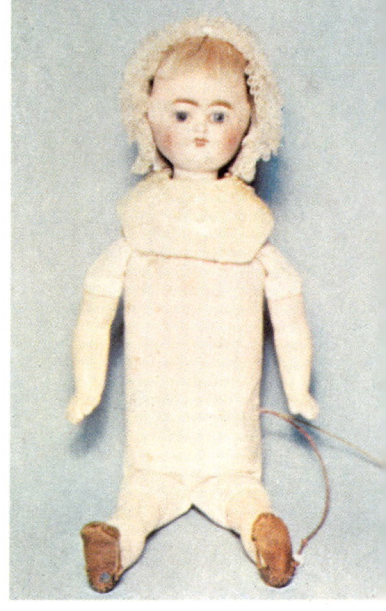

Double-faced doll made by Fritz Bartenstein, about 1890. Though unusual, it was originally cheaply produced, as the clothes and the doll's general construction are tawdry

German Dolls

During the middle years of the nineteenth century, German manufacturers had held a monopoly in the making of porcelain dolls' heads. The introduction of the *Bébé*-type doll in France, and the success of the French factories, such as Jumeau, which really made an effort to sell their products through intensive advertising, made the German manufacturers realize that they too would have to become innovators.

The German factories were able to produce less expensive dolls than the French, as they had a large number of lowly-paid workers at their disposal. In 1873 Fleischmann, for instance, is said to have had 32,000 employees! The low cost of the product meant that by the beginning of the twentieth century, many French firms were using German-made heads on dolls which they themselves assembled and dressed. The quality of the bisque used for the heads was excellent, and compared favourably with that used by the best French makers. The low price of the German-made dolls enabled even poor children to own them, and this has meant that thousands of German dolls are still available for the new collector.

The more interesting German dolls are those with character faces, whistling tongues, or sideways-moving eye mechanisms, known as 'flirting eyes'. Most common were the ordinary sleeping dolls, whose eyes were worked by a lead counter-weight mechanism. This was a German innovation, as the French dollmakers did not at first appear to like closing eyes on a doll. Black dolls are now popular among collectors, especially as they are becoming items of historical interest. As most new collectors begin by buying the less expensive examples, German dolls are dealt with here in rather more detail than the French, though in the last year the price gap between the two has narrowed considerably as German dolls are becoming more appreciated.

Pair of German bisque shoulder-headed dolls with leather bodies. The doll dressed as a lady was made by Simon & Halbig, while the doll in the straw hat was made by Armand Marseille and marked 'Mabel'

Armand Marseille

The firm of 'Armand Marseille' produced an almost incredible number of dolls, which were exported particularly to England and America. Their attractive, gentle features are rather more realistic than the heavy features of the dolls produced by the major French companies, and the vast number of surviving examples has meant that the price in general has remained low.

In the 1890s the company was known as makers of china dolls' heads, and many early examples have bisque shoulder heads mounted on gussetted, and often well articulated, leather bodies. These tall, slim, leather-bodied dolls were often dressed as women, and some look very attractive in late Victorian costume. The lower arms are usually made of bisque, but unfortunately the leg from the knee down was often covered with only poor quality cotton material which, all too often, has rotted away, allowing the sawdust to escape. Presumably this economic method was used to save money, as the legs would normally be covered by stockings. Composition limbs are also frequently found, sometimes attached to bodies of thick pink or white cotton.

The jointed dolls usually have well-made bodies of thick composition or sturdy wood, but other, poorer versions were made of a very thin composition, which has often become torn or broken. If beginning a collection with an example of the firm's work, it is advisable to buy a doll whose body, as well as the head, is in good condition. As there are so many examples to choose from, this should not be too difficult.

During the First World War, German dolls disappeared from the market, but by the 1920s Armand Marseille was again producing many dolls in the old manner. Though they usually look very Edwardian, it should be remembered that many of them were still being made by this firm until after 1925.

Two bisque-headed double-jointed dolls made by Armand Marseille. The doll in boy's clothes is really a girl doll and should be differentiated from genuine boy dolls with moulded hair. Both the illustrated dolls are in original clothes, though the 'boy' was probably dressed at home. The girl doll is exactly as it was when sold, as the father of the child to whom it was given nailed it into a case

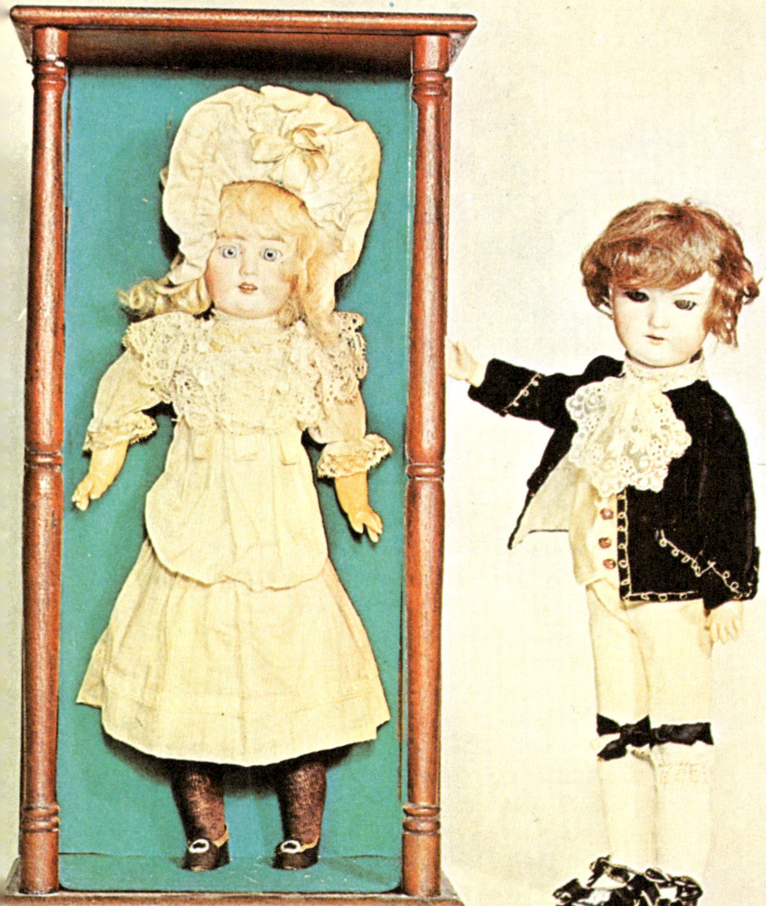

Bisque-headed Oriental baby doll made by Armand Marseille. Several slightly different heads were marketed by this firm, though the yellowish colour is better in some examples than in others

    A collector could choose perhaps one type of doll produced by Armand Marseille, and find enough examples to establish a very respectable group. Baby dolls were made in a wide variety of sizes and types. The smaller versions are usually much more attractive than the big ones, which always tend to look poorly modelled, though they are easy to dress, as Edwardian baby clothes fit them adequately.

    The black doll, which is illustrated, has a particularly attractive face, and the bisque is well tinted. Many black dolls had a rather unpleasant type of paint applied, which covered the texture of the bisque. Oriental babies were made in several different moulds, and the three in my collection are all different; the marks on their heads also vary. The bisque Oriental baby in the illustration was sold to me by a dealer in porcelain as a wax doll! It is in this lack of transference from one type of antique to another, that the collector often finds the opportunity to make good acquisitions.

European baby dolls are obviously much more common, but even among these there is variety, some heads having dimples and fixed intaglio eyes, while a few have crying expressions. One baby doll in my collection has a neat round hole, about the size of a penny, which was cut in the top of the head before the colour was added, and it was obviously quite intentional, though the reason why is elusive.

There is not quite as much variety among the heads of double-jointed dolls, but many, such as the two illustrated, are found beautifully dressed. The doll in the French-looking clothes in the display-case was bought ready-dressed and nailed into place through the back of the doll's body, over sixty years ago, so that the little girl who once owned her could see, but never touch (see page 121).

Attractive closed-mouth black bisque baby doll with curved limbs. This doll has a good soft colour. Later examples were sometimes painted black. The white baby is a very common Armand Marseille

Dark-skinned Simon & Halbig jointed girl doll, 14 ins. (36 cm.) high. Two strings lead from the back of the neck and work the eyes so they can remain open when the doll is lying down

Simon & Halbig

A few early Simon & Halbig dolls are to be found with bisque shoulder heads and moulded hair, similar to those which were popular in the middle of the nineteenth century, though the marked *S & H* dolls would appear by their hairstyles to date after 1875.

Like Armand Marseille, Simon & Halbig was a porcelain factory that included dolls' heads among its products, though they made a far greater variety of types than Armand Marseille. Many of the German dolls' heads which were exported to France and used on French bodies, were made by Simon & Halbig. They were used even on Jumeau bodies despite Jumeau's protestations that they produced all parts of the dolls themselves.

Simon & Halbig heads were also used on the Edison phonograph dolls, which could recite nursery rhymes, and on bodies with walking mechanisms made by Roullet & Decamps. Besides exporting dolls' heads for use in France and America, the firm also supplied heads to other German companies, so that some heads are found with both the names of Heinrich Handwerck and Simon & Halbig, though most were made for Kämmer and Reinhardt.

Except in the case of the shoulder-headed dolls, the heads made by this firm are very clearly marked, which makes their attribution fairly simple.

Several different eye mechanisms are commonly found, the baby doll in the illustration having sideways glancing eyes, which move to the opposite side when the doll is turned. The brown-faced double-jointed girl doll has eyes that open and close by the pulling of strings, which lead out from two small

Another interesting eye mechanism used by Simon & Halbig was the 'flirty eye' movement. The eyes move from side to side as the doll is turned. This version also cries 'mama'. Accepted as a 'character' doll

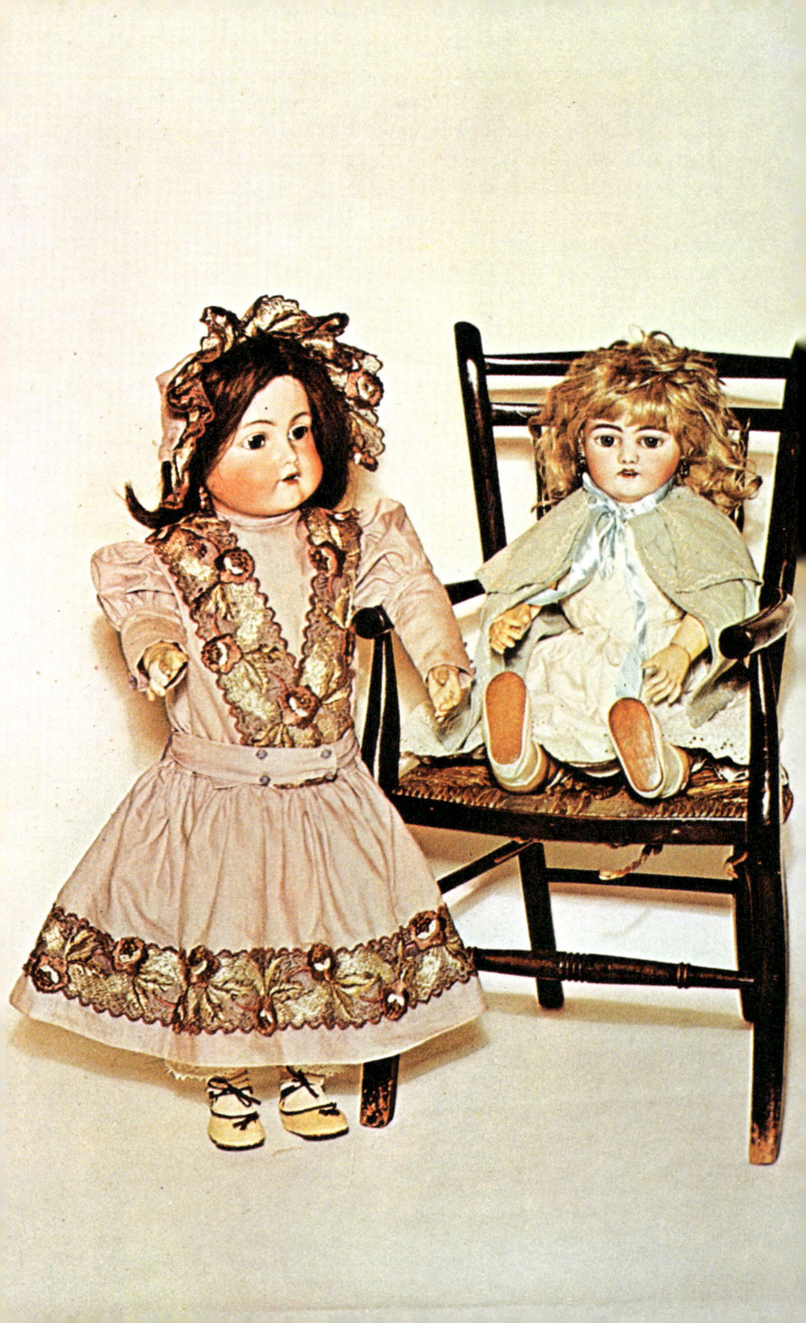

holes in the back of the head. Though the brown girl doll is silent, the white baby cries 'mama' when tilted.

Several attractive lady dolls' heads were marketed by Simon & Halbig, the bodies of a few having a much more realistic shape than is usually found on dolls of the period, looking, in fact, very like many of the teenage-type dolls sold today. The traditional leather body often carried a rather lady-like head, as did others of cloth; both types usually had lower arms quite well modelled in bisque.

The heads made by Simon & Halbig compare very favourably in quality with those made in France, as the bisque is often of a much better quality. The pierced ears, which the dolls often have, make them especially attractive. Many, such as the doll in the blue cape, which is illustrated, look very like the products of the S.F.B.J. company, while other, more interesting examples, could be taken for Jumeaus.

Japanese, Indian, Burmese and Chinese dolls, and black and brown bisques were made, as well as other white dolls which were intended for dressing in regional costume. A Dutch girl doll has clogs moulded on the composition legs, for example, while a French peasant doll might have black boots.

Apart from manufacturing china head dolls, the company also made heads of composition and celluloid, though the substance of both these types has meant that they are usually in a poor state of preservation.

The voice-boxes which the firm used are often very primitive. The torso was sometimes roughly cut in two, the voice-box inserted, and the two halves glued together after a square had been cut away and covered with wire gauze to allow the escape of sound. So crude is the method of fixing, that the impression is often erroneously given that the voice-box has been added to the doll at a later date.

Simon & Halbig dolls were usually better finished than the products of many of the other German makers and the firm experimented with an unusually large range of mechanisms. The two dolls illustrated are typical of the quality dolls produced by the firm until 1925. The standing doll was bought in Kilburn High Street, London, by a nurse for her young sister in 1912

A pair of leather-bodied dolls with bisque heads and arms made by the firm of Cuno & Otto Dressel, about 1895. Both have sleeping eyes. Clowns from the Schoenhut Circus and Victorian children's books

S.P.B.H. and Dressel

The fact that Schoenau and Hoffmeister marked their dolls with and *S* and *H* on either side of a star, often causes new collectors to confuse the dolls with the products of the Simon & Halbig factory. The *P.B.* which is written in the centre of the star, stands for Porzellanfabrik Burggrub. A date also often appears on the heads of dolls made by this firm, which is probably related to the date when the mould was first introduced. Double-jointed and baby dolls were made, and a few character-type heads, such as a yellow tinted Oriental bisque. Several dolls of this make are found that have been very badly painted at home, and versions appear to have been sold in the white. These often look rather horrific with the home-applied paint peeling off. The jointed girl dolls have very beautiful faces, often enhanced by the combination of enormous brown eyes with blonde hair.

Cuno & Otto Dressel were founded in 1700 in Sonneberg, and presumably made toys of papier-mâché, wood and porcelain, which were typical of the area. Being toymakers rather than purely dollmakers, they marketed dolls with heads made by several different companies, so that at times the modelling and bisque is excellent, while at other times it is of very poor quality. A similar disparity of standard exists in the construction of the bodies. The doll dressed as a boy, which is illustrated, has a well-made and shaped body, while the girl doll in brown has a figure that leaves much to be desired!

The firm marketed dolls in a variety of substances, from the composition which they had made since their inception, to poured wax heads, often mounted on leather bodies. The most common are the bisque heads, though by 1910 the firm was making jointed dolls, babies, and dolls of celluloid.

Large jointed bisque doll with the attractive face typical of the products of the Schoenau & Hoffmeister factory. Head marked S.P.B.H. This doll was known as 'Queenie' by her former owner

Other German Makers

Many German firms which manufactured dolls' heads also made good-quality porcelain. Armand Marseille, for instance, made quite pretty porcelain figures in the typical style of the period. The Limbach Porzellanfabrik made the very pale-faced doll dressed as a lady, which is illustrated. The bisque of this doll's head is much thinner than usual, which possibly accounts for the few of this type that have survived, though other heads made by the firm and marked '*Wally*' are more thickly moulded and appear to be found in greater numbers.

The Rauenstein Porzellanfabrik also made good-quality dolls' heads; one which looks very like a French doll is on a body that could have come straight from the Jumeau factory, though others are found on very obviously German bodies.

The doll dressed in a maid's uniform was produced by the company of Charles Bergmann, which, like most of the other makers, chiefly manufactured ball-jointed dolls. This firm did not make their dolls' heads themselves, but bought them from other makers, such as Simon & Halbig, and merely assembled the product.

There were hundreds of small German firms which produced dolls, and examples are many times found which are difficult to attribute, although continual research goes on. In America, in particular, the Coleman family has conducted painstaking research into patents and designs (see *Books to Read* at end of book).

The Kubelka factory is interesting, as it obtained a patent for the insertion of a wax disc into an indentation in the head. The hair could then be rooted into this wax in a similar way to that used in the old wax dolls.

Among the more commonly found dolls are those made by Handwerck, Heubach, and Bruno Schmidt, the latter making dolls in celluloid, as well as bisque.

A very pale-coloured bisque jointed doll made at the Limbach porcelain factory, better known for fine china than dolls' heads. The jointed doll dressed as a maid with the rather highly coloured face was made by the Bergmann Factory, though it is thought that the Bergmann heads were made for the firm to assemble by Simon & Halbig and Armand Marseille

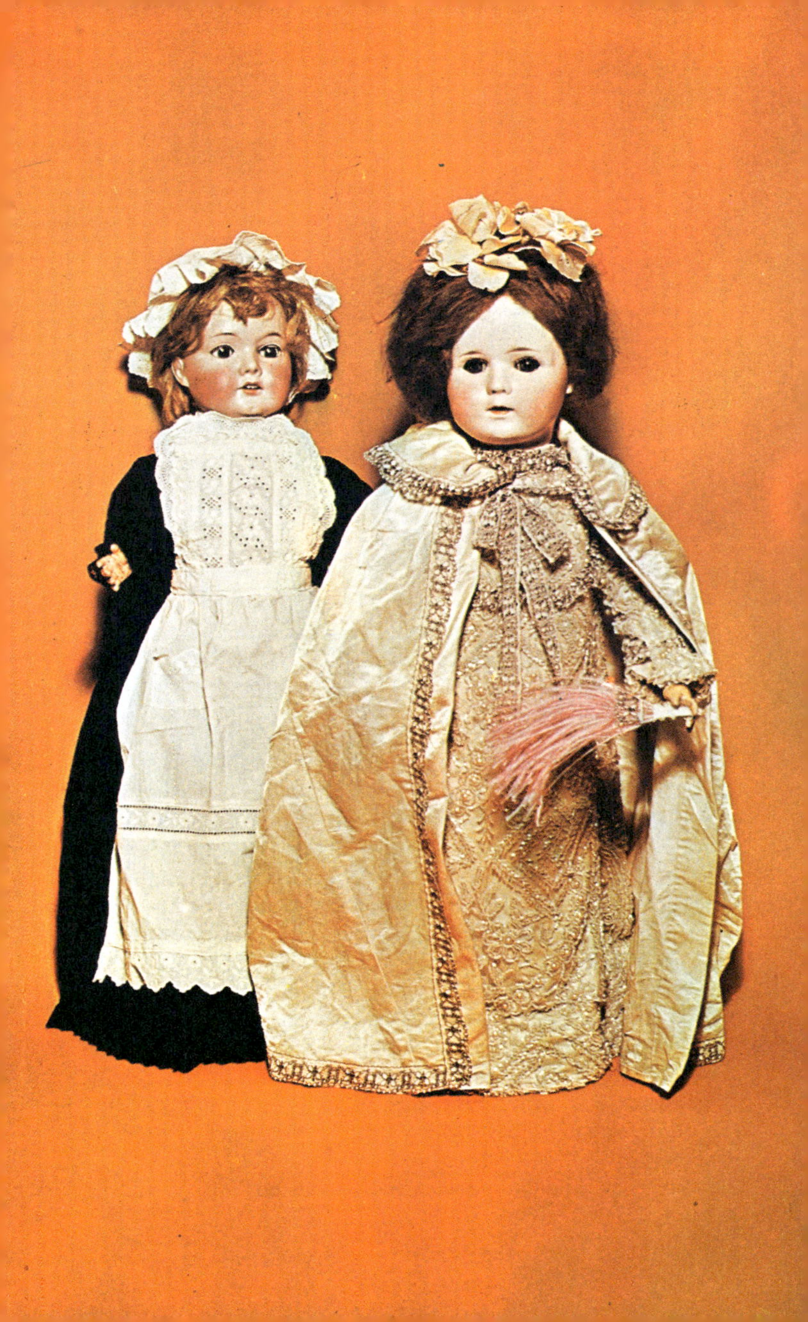

Sarah Thrifty, Licensed Hawker, about 1820. This wooden pedlar doll offers a variety of well-made items for sale. Probably home-made

Pedlar Dolls

The Pedlars appear to have been a particularly English type of doll, and many give the appearance of having been ladies' follies rather than children's playthings, especially examples such as the lady at a bazaar stall, on show at the Bethnal Green Museum in London, who is obviously performing her own little elegant duty to society, with a table loaded with bric-a-brac.

Hawkers often carried inexpensive dolls and toys to village children in the eighteenth and early nineteenth centuries. Being carriers of good things, as well as exciting news, it is little wonder that pedlars were created out of any type of doll that was available. They were usually dressed by the parent or nurse-maid, who also made many of the small objects which the dolls carried.

Very early pedlars are made of wood, but it is more usual to find these dolls made of wax – often the slit-headed type of doll, whose cracked face now gives the model great character. A dried apple fixed to a stick torso could also create a very realistically wrinkled old crone.

John Noble, of the Museum of the City of New York, mentions the existence of two pedlar dolls that are identical and yet came from different sources, suggesting that such dolls could be bought ready-made.

The value and interest of a doll of this type depends on the number of items displayed for sale. A doll whose basket is full of bits of lace and balls of wool is obviously of less interest than one that carried miniature sewing or kitchen equipment, books or dolls, which are amusing objects in their own right. As a large number of faked pedlars exist, it is advisable to examine the doll for sale carefully before buying, and to avoid any whose wares look recently arranged.

An effective papier-mâché pedlar doll, offering a good assortment of wares for sale from a tray. About 1835

Bent-limbed celluloid boy doll 14 ins. (35 cm.) high, with painted eyes, made by the Rheinische Gummi und Celluloid Fabrik Gesellschaft, about 1920

Rubber, Tin and Celluloid Dolls' Heads

The indestructible dolls' head was the ideal of the nineteenth-century dollmakers, and they were prepared to make use of any new invention to further that aim. Both German and French dollmakers produced dolls made of rubber, gutta-percha, tin and celluloid – products which appear to us as quaint and rather ugly specimens of firms that normally produced fine work.

Gutta-percha heads were often sold as joke novelties, with faces which became grotesque when squeezed, though the substance was also quite often combined with rubber, in an attempt to give a better finish. Rubber shoulder heads mounted on cloth bodies were produced as well as dolls made completely of rubber, but as they are usually found in bad condition – the material has often dried and cracked – they appear only rarely in collections. Many of the dolls were well moulded and, when new, must have looked as attractive as their china counterparts.

Metal heads must have appeared to the dollmakers as their ultimate dream – almost completely unbreakable – but they were never able to perfect a finish that would not chip, so that, like the rubber dolls, the metal examples are often badly disfigured. A good all-steel doll was made by the Metal Doll Company of New Jersey, having set-in glass eyes and a choice of wigs. Broken bisque heads were sometimes replaced by tin, so that it is often quite difficult to know whether the head is original.

Celluloid heads were introduced in the 1860s, continual improvements being made in an attempt to rid the heads of their over-glossy look, and to minimize fading. Most of the dollmakers experimented with celluloid, but these dolls are only worth buying today, if they are in good condition, as they are very difficult to repair.

Tin head, about 1920. Such heads were sometimes used as replacements for china heads, though some were mounted on metal or composition bodies

Closed-mouth Heubach baby doll with painted intaglio eyes. A particularly attractive baby mould. 9 ins. (23 cm.) high

Character Dolls

A character doll has features that are not idealized but are represented as they might be on a child, with wrinkles, tears and, quite often, an ugly expression. The demand for more realistic dolls became stronger after 1910, and a wide range of character dolls was produced. Artists were often commissioned to model a head as a portrait of an actual child or baby, though the identity of these children is usually lost. Advertisements issued by Kämmer & Reinhardt, do, however, survive, and many of the dolls are illustrated accompanied by names which are believed to be those of the children who posed, such as Peter, Marie, Gretchen or Carl. These double-jointed dolls were sold alongside the bent-limb baby dolls, which were becoming increasingly popular by the 1920s. The pair of baby dolls illustrated is of a boy and girl version of a similar character doll. These babies are hardly pretty, but a doll made by the Heubach factory, depicting a child having a tantrum, is even more cruelly realistic!

Louis Amberg made a bisque-headed baby, modelled on a three-day old infant, while other interesting characters were made by firms such as Armand Marseille, Kestner, Simon & Halbig, and Kley & Hahn.

The French factories had been overtaken by the German in the production of dolls before character models became really popular, and consequently far fewer are to be found, though Jumeau made a character girl called 'Mirette' and S.F.B.J. and Steiner both produced attractive coloured jointed dolls.

Adults such as 'Old Ripp' and 'Uncle Sam' were made, as well as lady dolls, such as one made by Armand Marseille, which had a particularly life-like face.

Conventional mass-produced dolls are often labelled 'characters' and, as the borderline between the two is very fine, it is sometimes useful to ask yourself: 'Does this doll really look like a child?'.

Two character dolls 11 ins. (28 cm.) high. The boy marked K ✱ R and the girl K ✱ R and Simon & Halbig. The girl has sleeping eyes; the boy's eyes are painted

THE TWENTIETH CENTURY

An interesting social phenomenon of the early twentieth century was the re-emergence of dolls specifically aimed at the adult market. Often called 'Boudoir' or 'Art' dolls, these rather fashionable ladies have very tall bodies and elegant, rather haughty features, painted on plaster, cotton or silk. As the colour has faded, dolls of this type often look much older than they really are. Wax dolls of a similar type were also made, many being intended as nightdress-cases or telephone-covers. In the 1920s Bernard Ravca of Paris made art dolls in imitation of interesting characters, which are reminiscent of paintings by Toulouse-Lautrec and which have tremendous period charm.

The effect of the cinema on toy production became very marked in the 1930s, so that characters such as Charlie Chaplin were made. Shirley Temple dolls were also very popular, as was Mickey Mouse, who adapted to a very successful soft toy.

A boudoir doll of the 1920s, dressed in fashionable lounging pyjamas, and a velvet and felt Micky Mouse with long rubber tail

The Golliwog, popular both as a soft toy and as a character in children's books. Created by Florence Upton in 1895

Kewpie all-bisque baby dolls, with their characteristic upswept hair and enormous eyes, became very fashionable among adults as well as children. The doll was designed in 1912 in the United States by Rose O'Neill and manufactured by several German porcelain factories. The Kewpie was collectable even when new, as it was produced to represent various occupations such as firemen, soldiers and farmers. In 1925 'Scootles' was designed by the same lady, to succeed the Kewpie, but it never became as popular.

Many of the china dolls made at the time were at least partly based on the idea of a doll that was half toy, half ornament, and they often look very strange when an effort is made to dress them.

Though the Golliwog was created in 1895 by Florence Upton in her book, *The Adventures of Two Dutch Dolls and a Golliwog,* it really became popular as a soft toy in the twentieth century. Early Golliwogs can be recognized by their noses, which were made to protrude slightly, and they are much more frightening than the modern, simplified versions.

A much loved and well travelled Teddy Bear made in the 1920s. His pointed nose is less emphasized than it would be on an earlier bear. Straw-filled

Teddy Bears

Controversy has raged as to the country of origin of the Teddy Bear since it first appeared in the toy world in 1903. It is popularly believed to have originated in America, but while the American manufacturer was still producing bears in a very small way, the German company of Frau Margarete Steiff accepted an American order for 3,000 bears at the Leipzig Fair in 1903, and by 1907 over one million bears a year were being exported from Germany.

The bear was based on a bear cub in a cartoon by Clifford Berryman, which showed Teddy Roosevelt after a hunt in the Rocky Mountains, with a little brown cub in the background. Morris Michton, the proprietor of a small shop in Brooklyn, which sold some hand-made toys, was inspired to produce a toy of brown plush in imitation of the bear he had seen in the cartoon. His wife at first helped sew the toys which they sold from their shop, but so great was their popularity, that out of this small beginning grew The Ideal Toy Corporation of America.

The tragedy of the Teddy Bear for the collector is that it has usually been overloved and is often in poor condition after being inexpertly mended. Early bears usually have a long, almost fox-like, pointed nose and fairly small ears, the German version in particular having a thin body. Many home-made examples exist which can really only be dated by reference to the maker. The early bears were made in a variety of fabrics, from a smooth plush, to quite luxuriant, long shaggy coats, though in the latter case the face was left with a short pile to show up the features. The nose was often stitched along its length, rather than being simply indicated with large black stitches as it is today.

A very large bear with leather paws, made in the early 1930s, and the author's own beloved 'Rupert', made by Chad Valley in the 1940s

Model theatre, about 1910, with early nineteenth-century figures. The theatre was probably home-made to display the characters

PLACES TO VISIT

In Britain
Bethnal Green Museum, London
British Museum, London
Gunnersbury Park Museum, London
The Horniman Museum, London
The London Museum, London
Pollocks' Toy Museum, London
Victoria & Albert Museum, London
Windsor Castle, Windsor
Barry Elder Doll Museum, Preston

Birmingham Museum and Art Gallery, Birmingham
City Museum, Leeds
Abbey House Museum, Kirkstall, Leeds
Art Gallery and Museum, Keighley
Warwick Doll Museum, Warwick
Fitzwilliam Museum, Cambridge
Cambridge and County Folk Museum, Cambridge
The Grange Toy Museum, Rottingdean
The Holly Trees Museum, Colchester
Museum and Art Gallery, Luton
Saffron Walden Museum, Saffron Walden
Royal Tunbridge Wells Museum and Art Gallery, Tunbridge Wells
Worthing Museum and Art Gallery, Worthing
The Rotunda, Oxford (adults only)
American Museum in Britain, Bath
Welsh Folk Museum, Cardiff
Penrhyn Castle, Bangor
The Museum of Childhood, Edinburgh

In America
Children's Museum, Brooklyn, New York
The Museum of the City of New York, New York
Detroit Public Schools Children's Museum, Detroit
The Henry Ford Museum, Dearborn
Essex Institute, Salem (Mass.)
Plymouth Antiquarian Society, Plymouth
Mary Merritt's Doll Museum, Douglasville
Smithsonian Institution, Washington D.C.
Wisconsin State Historical Society, Madison
Winterthur Museum, Winterthur

In Europe
Musée des Arts Décoratifs, Paris
Musée d'Histoire de l'Education, Paris
Bayerisches Nationalmuseum, Munich
Germanisches Nationalmuseum, Nuremberg
Deutsches Spielzeugmuseum, Sonneberg
Städtische Kunstsammlungen, Augsburg
Nordiska Museet, Stockholm
Dansk Folkemuseum, Copenhagen
Norsk Folkemuseum, Oslo
National Museum of Finland, Helsinki
Haags Gemeentemuseum, The Hague
Rijksmuseum, Amsterdam

Two all-china dolls made in the 1920s, with a bathroom set of a similar date. The Kewpie-type doll was made in Germany

DOLLS' MARKS
German Makers

K ⊠&⊠ R	Kämmer & Reinhardt, Waltershausen, 1886–1928
made in ℱ. Germany. 10 211 J.D.K. J.D.K. 🐢	J. D. Kestner, Waltershausen, 1805–1925+
⟩K&H⟨ Germany J 169-9 J	Kley and Hahn, Ohrdruf, 1895–1925+
👑 (Limbach crown mark)	Limbach Porcelain Factory, Limbach, 1772–1925+
SCHUTZ MARKE 🐢	Rheinische Gummi und Celluloid Fabrik Co., Mannheim-Neckarau, 1873–1925+

144

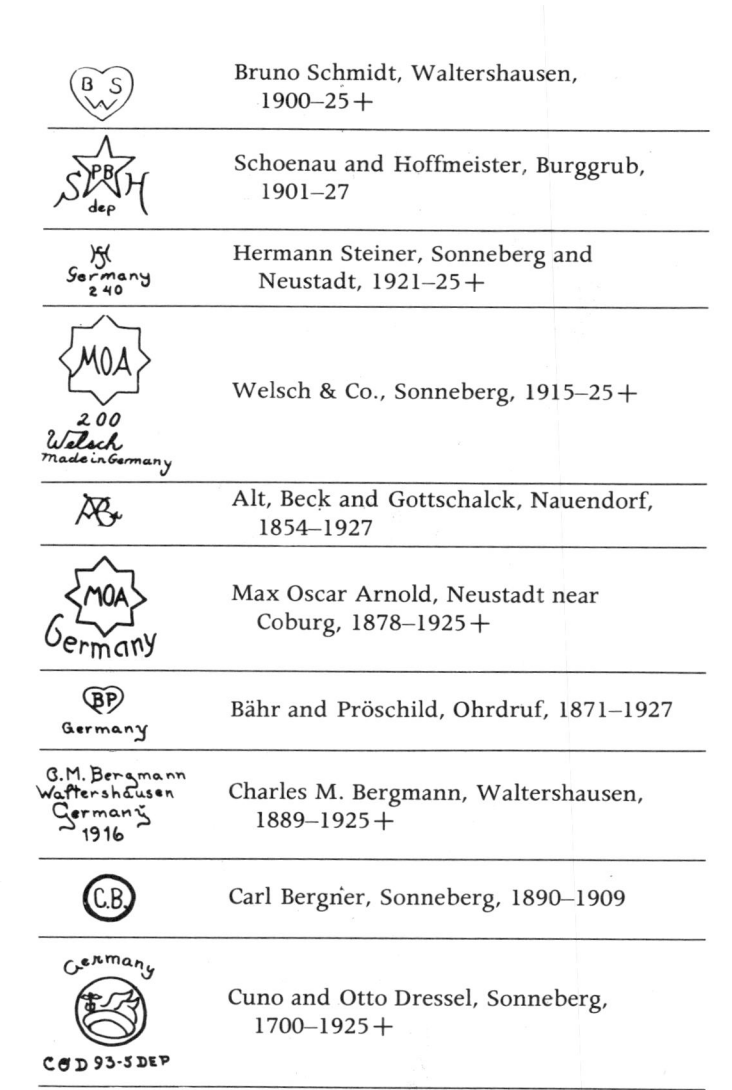

Mark	Description
(BS / W in heart)	Bruno Schmidt, Waltershausen, 1900–25+
S PB H (star) dep	Schoenau and Hoffmeister, Burggrub, 1901–27
HS / Germany / 240	Hermann Steiner, Sonneberg and Neustadt, 1921–25+
MOA (star) / 200 / Welsch / Made in Germany	Welsch & Co., Sonneberg, 1915–25+
ABG	Alt, Beck and Gottschalck, Nauendorf, 1854–1927
MOA (star) / Germany	Max Oscar Arnold, Neustadt near Coburg, 1878–1925+
BP / Germany	Bähr and Pröschild, Ohrdruf, 1871–1927
C.M. Bergmann / Waftershausen / Germany / 1916	Charles M. Bergmann, Waltershausen, 1889–1925+
C.B.	Carl Bergner, Sonneberg, 1890–1909
Germany / (crest) / C&D 93-5 DEP	Cuno and Otto Dressel, Sonneberg, 1700–1925+
A ELLAR M (star) / Germany	'Ellar' marks on Armand Marseille baby dolls, c. 1925

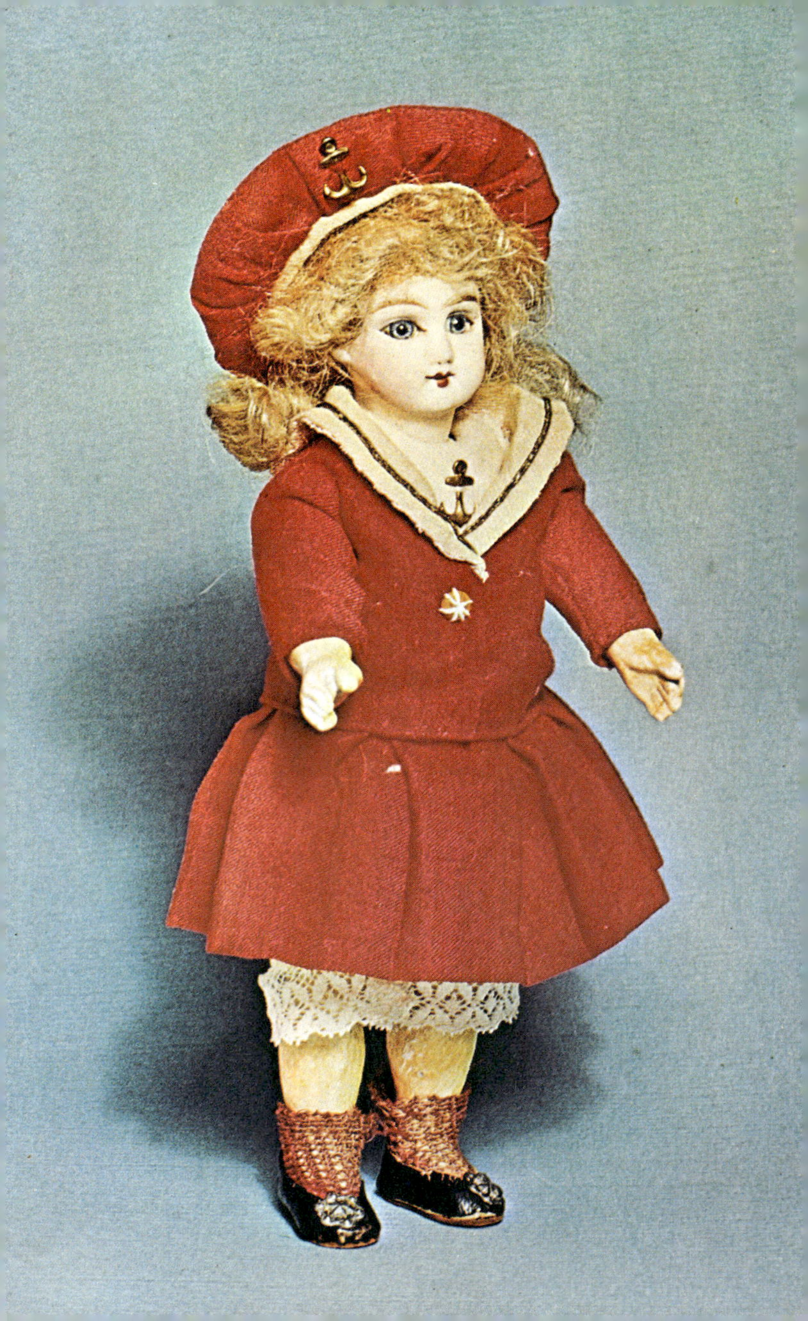

P⚹F	Arno Fischer, Ilmenau, 1907–1925+
ℜ - n	Rauenstein Porcelain Factory, Thür, founded in 1783
HANDWERCK .H.)¹(	Marks on dolls made by Heinrich Handwerck, Gotha, 1902–25+
Heubach-Köppelsdorf 250·15/0 ˢ Germany (🐎H K 0)	Marks found on dolls made by Ernst Heubach, Köppelsdorf, 1887–1925+

Armand Marseille, Köppelsdorf, 1865–1930

ArmandMarseille Germany 990 A 9/0 M Armand Marseille Germany 390 A 11/0 M	most commonly found marks
Germany 550 A 3 M D.R.G.M	mark found on closed-mouth character head
ArmandMarseille Germany 401 A 5/0 M	mark found on adult character head
Germany. 370 A 6 M	mark usually found on shoulder heads
590 A. 5 M. Germany D.R.G.M.	mark found on character bisque-head dolls with 'open-closed' mouth
3200 A.M 8/0 DEP	mark c. 1899
1894 A.M. 0 D.E.P. Made in Germany	another common mark

French doll dressed in Victorian-style sailor suit. About 1900

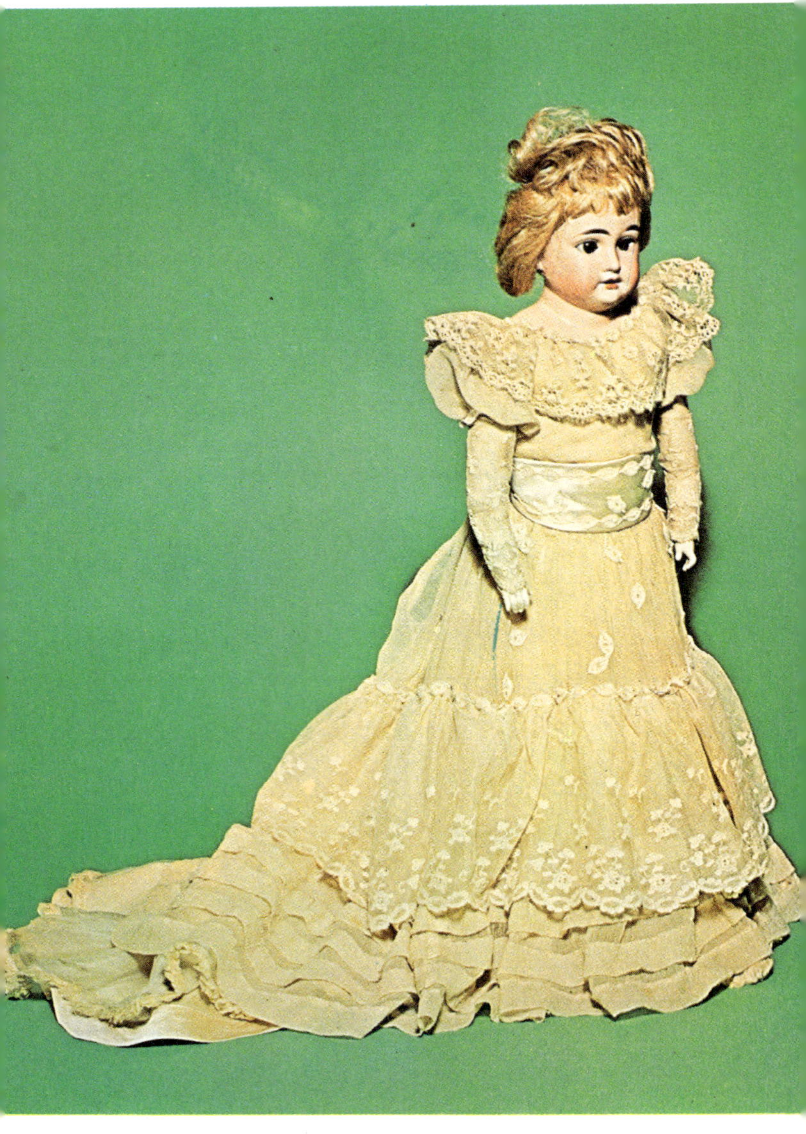

Simon and Halbig, Gräfenhain, 1870–1927

Mark	Description
S & K	trademark of firm
SIMON & HALBIG S & H IV	character face
S H 1039 4 DEP	found on brown bisque-head dolls
K ✡ R SIMON & HALBIG 122	heads made by Simon and Halbig for Kämmer and Reinhart
1299 SIMON & HALBIG 3½	bisque-head dolls with character face
1079-2 DEP S H Germany 1008 SIMON & HALBIG S & H K ✡ R SIMON & HALBIG HALBIG K ✹ R Germany 17 S 14 H 949	some other marks

Cuno & Otto Dressel doll dressed in Edwardian wedding-dress. 1895

Two jointed dolls typical of those made at the beginning of the century. Small doll marked *S.F.B.J.* Larger doll German

French Makers

BÉBÉ-COIFFURE	Guttmann & Schiffnie, 1897–1925+
⌒ ⊙ BRU	Marks used by Bru Jne. & Cie., Paris, 1866–99
DL	Mark used by Louis Delachal for rubber dolls, Paris, 1890–1904
EDEN-BÉBÉ	Mark used by Fleischmann & Bloedel, Paris, 1909–25+
AL & Cie LIMOGES	Lanternier & Cie., Limoges, 1855–1925+
G D	Grandjean, Paris, 1887–90
HURET	Maison Huret, Paris, 1850–1920
JUMEAU MEDAILLE D'OR PARIS DÉPOSE TÊTE JUMEAU	Marks used by Jumeau, Paris, 1842–99

J P	Jacob Petit, Fontainebleau, 1830–62
R.4.D	Rabery & Delphieu, Paris, 1856–98
(shield with SCH)	Schmitt, Paris, 1863–91
(PARIS S.F. DEPOSÉ)	Schneider, Paris, 1858–96
S.F.B.J. PARIS	Société de Fabrication de Bébés & Jouets, Paris, 1899–1925+
STEINER .S.G.D.G. PARIS AII	Jules Nicholas Steiner, Paris, 1855–91

Doll 22 ins. (60 cm.) high, made by Armand Marseille in about 1910. This particular doll was once a display model for children's clothes

Other Makers

L.A.S. 414 1911	Louis Amberg doll importer and maker, New York, 1878–81
GOSS 30	Goss and Company, Stoke-on-Trent, 1858–1925
GREINER'S IMPROVED PATENTHEADS	Ludwig Greiner, Philadelphia, 1840–74
MADE IN U.S.A. MARKS BROTHERS CO BOSTON	Marks Bros. Co., Boston, 1918–25+
FROM E. MOODY SOHO BAZAAR / CHAS. MARSH SOLE MANUFACTURER LONDON / DOLLS CLEANED & REPAIRED	William Marsh, London, 1865–1914
H.J. MEECH DOLL MAKER DOLLS CLEANED & REPAIRED 50 KENNINGTON ROAD LONDON S.E.1	H. J. Meech, London, 1865–91 (on wax and composition dolls)
Montanari 180 Soho Bazaar London	Montanari, London, 1851–84
Pierotti	Pierotti family, London, 1780–1930
S	Strobel and Wilken, Ohio and New York, 1864–1925+

REPAIRING AND FAKES

I was surprised recently to be offered a fake German leather-bodied doll by what appeared to be quite honest people. Though French fashion dolls and Jumeaus have been reproduced for some time, one is unprepared for the faking of the much lower-priced German dolls. The fact that the leather underneath the old clothes was fresh and white, and the bisque of the head rather highly coloured, exposed the deceit, but the bisque was of an extremely fine quality.

If a dolls' house or doll is owned which is in bad condition, it is normally better to leave it alone. An inexperienced restorer can create irreparable damage to a clockwork mechanism or the face of a doll. Composition dolls are particularly difficult to clean, and many museums have examples on show which have suffered badly in the hands of a restorer. It is far better to leave a doll dirty rather than to risk ruining it, unless it is made of china, in which case it can be washed carefully. Over-zealous restorers can often spoil dolls' houses in an attempt to make them look pretty. Old wallpapers are sometimes stripped out and ugly modern wrapping papers substituted, and the woodwork is painted with gloss paint. As with any antique, it is well to remember that one is, after all, its owner for only a relatively short time, and every effort should be made to preserve a toy in its original state for as long as possible.

GLOSSARY

Art dolls, dolls designed by artists. Also used to refer to lady dolls of the twentieth century
Bald heads, dolls' heads made without hair for a wig to be attached
Ball joint, method of articulating two parts of the body with a wooden ball
Bank money-boxes, made by post office and other savings banks who hold the keys
Biedermeier dolls, early nineteenth-century dolls with black spot on crown of head
Biskoline, substance similar to celluloid
Bisque, unglazed porcelain
Bonnet dolls, dolls with headdress moulded in one with head
Celluloid, synthetic material composed of cellulose nitrate, camphor, pigments and alcohol
Character dolls, dolls that resemble an actual person
Dep., *Deponiert* (German) or *Deposé* (French), indicates a registered design or trade mark
Duncan Phyfe furniture, term coined by Vivian Greene to describe dolls' house furniture in imitation rosewood
Edible toys, made of substances such as gum tragacanth,

gingerbread or barley sugar
Elastolin, trade name for composition substance used for modelling
Flange necks, necks that open out at lower edge to be held in place by cloth bodies
Flirting eyes, American term for dolls' eyes that move from side to side
Froebel toys, a series of toys which taught skills based on Froebel's educational theories
Frozen Charlottes, glazed porcelain dolls with fixed arms and legs
Gesso, fine plaster used for giving good surface to wooden heads
Gutta-percha, elastic substance obtained from Malaya
Happifats, dolls based on drawings by Kate Jordan. German made, after 1914
Hottentots, black Kewpies made from 1915
Milliners' Models, term coined by Eleanor St George to describe papier-mâché heads with moulded hair
Open-closed mouths, mouths parted to show tongue or teeth but no actual entry into head
Pandoras, large fashion models
Pantin, a jumping jack
Parian, fine dense white hard-paste or soft-paste porcelain invented during the 1840s
Pate, crown of head
Phenakisticope, optical toy giving illusion of movement when viewed through a mirror
Polyoptic pictures, distorted figures which, when viewed in a polished metal cylinder, appear normal
Poupards, dolls mounted on a stick. A tune is played when stick is twisted
Pouties, American term for dolls with pouting expression
Sand toys, pictures activated by trickling sand
Scarf dolls, dolls with scarf or turban moulded with head
Slit heads, wax dolls' heads with a cut across top for insertion of hair
Stereoscope, a viewer which gives a three-dimensional effect to photographs
Swivel necks, heads that turn in socket at base of neck

Velocipede, any three-wheeled bicycle-type toy
Walker-Izannah F., American rag dolls with paste-stiffened faces
Whistling dolls, dolls with mouth puckered to whistle when body is squeezed
Winking dolls, dolls made between 1910 and 1920 with one eye closed and smiling mouth

ACKNOWLEDGEMENTS

By Gracious Permission of Her Majesty the Queen 82, 83
Author's Collection 21, 23, 27, 28, 31, 32, 33 (right), 34, 36, 37, 42, 45–47, 52–57, 60–63, 66, 70, 71, 72 (right), 74–77, 81, 84, 85, 89, 92, 94–101, 103–105, 107, 108, 110, 112, 114, 117–119, 121–129, 131, 134–139, 141, 144, 153, back cover
Basset-Lowke Ltd., London 41
Bethnal Green Museum, London 14, 15, 17, 19, 73, 79
Mrs K. Brott 33 (left)
Christie, Manson & Woods, London 88
City of Manchester Art Galleries 10, 102, 132
City of Norwich Museums 12, 13
Colchester and Essex Museum 44, 58, 133
Cooper-Bridgeman Library 41, 86, 88
Robert Culff Collection 86
Lt Peter Edwards 35 (left)
Gaby Goldscheider 24, 26, 29, 30, 35 (right), 68, 69, 72 (left), 142
Green's Antique Galleries, London 90, 91
Guildhall Museum, London 5, 7
Horniman Museum, London 4
Lord Chamberlain's Office 82, 83
Mrs J. Marsh 146, 148, 150
Museum of Childhood, Edinburgh 67
Penshurst Place Toy Museum, Kent 64, 78, front cover
Pollocks' Toy Museum, London 43, 48, 49, 50, 51, 87
Miss Georgina Pritchard 140
Mrs K. Reddick 151
Mrs H. Sebastian 54
Trustees of the British Museum 9
Trustees of the London Museum, Kensington Palace 6, 16, 18, 22, 25, 38, 39, 40, title page
Worthing Museum, Sussex 59

BOOKS TO READ

Model Soldiers by Massimo Alberini. Orbis Books, London, 1972.

Dolls and Puppets by Max von Böhn. Harrap, London, 1932.

Movement in Two Dimensions by Olive Cook. Hutchinson, London, 1963.

The Collector's Encyclopedia of Dolls by Dorothy, Elizabeth and Evelyn Coleman. Crown, New York, 1968.

The World of Toys by Robert Culff. Hamlyn, London, 1969.

Children's Toys Throughout the Ages by Lesley Daiken. Batsford, London, 1953.

Dolls and Dolls' Houses by Kay Desmonde. Letts, London, 1972.

Dolls, A New Guide for Collectors by Claire Hallard Fawcett. Branford, New York, 1964.

A History of Toys by Antonia Fraser. Weidenfeld & Nicolson, London, 1966.

A Collector's Guide to Model Soldiers by John G. Garratt. Seeley Service, London, 1959.

The Dolls of Yesterday by Eleanor St George. Scribner, New York, 1948.

Old Dolls by Eleanor St George. Barrows, New York, 1950.

English Dolls' Houses of the Eighteenth and Nineteenth Centuries by Vivian Greene. Batsford, London, 1955.

Children's Toys of Bygone Days by Karl Gröber. Batsford, London, 1928.

Dolls and Dollmakers by Mary Hillier. Weidenfeld & Nicolson, London, 1968.

A History of Doll's Houses by Flora Gill Jacobs. Cassell, London, 1956.

Dolls' Houses. A Personal Choice by Jean Latham. A & C. Black, London, 1969.

Antiques in Miniature by Katharine McClinton. Barrie and Jenkins, London, 1972.

Toys by Patrick Murray. Studio Vista, London, 1968.

Dolls by John Noble. Studio Vista, London, 1968.

Antique Miniature Furniture in Great Britain and America by Jane Toller. Bell, London, 1966.

European and American Dolls by Gwen White. Batsford, London, 1966.

Dolls of the World by Gwen White. Mills & Boon, London, 1962.

The Collector's Book of Children's Books by Eric Quaile. Studio Vista, London, 1971.

INDEX

Figures in bold type refer to illustrations

Acrobatic toys 86–7; **86, 87**
Adventures of Two Dutch Dolls and a Golliwog, The 139
Albert, Prince 32
America 11, 12, 15, 20, 34, 36, 40, 42–3, 50, 55, 62, 66, 70, 73, 77–9, 86–7, 103, 115, 130, 139, 140–1
Animals, Toy 17, 60; **60, 61**
Animated books 27
Anne, Queen 11
Annuals 27
Apprentice pieces 72; **72**
Armand Marseille 120, 124 130, 137; **119, 121, 122, 123, 151**
'Art' Dolls 138
Asalto board **68**
Augsburg 48, 78
Automata 17, 89, 90; **88, 90, 91**
Autoperipatetikos 91

Baby dolls 122, 125, 136, 139; **103, 122, 136**
Baby Houses 8, 12, 14, 74, 80; **10, 14**
Baby walkers 59, 60; **59**
Bagman's Baby 93
Balloons, miniature 17
Balls 4
Bassett-Lowke 42
Bébés 113, 116, 118; **112**
Beds, Toy 84–5; **84**
Bentwood furniture 77
Bergmann, Charles 130; **130**
Berryman, Clifford 140
Bethnal Green Museum 83, 132
Bing, Gebrüder 43; **41**
Bisques 94, 106, 109, 124, 127, 129–30; **106, 117, 119, 121, 122, 123, 128, 129, 130**
'Black Prince' 42
Blackett House, The 15
Blow Point 16
Boats 5, 58, 66–67; **36**
Boats, Rocking 66–67; **66**
Boats, Swinging 58
'Bonnet' dolls 106
Book of Martyrs 25
Books, Children's 6, 17, 20, 24–27
'Boudoir' dolls 138; **138**
Bows and arrows 16

Boy dolls 106; **106, 137**
Britain, William 47; **45**
Bru 109, 111, 113, 115; **113**
Building bricks 31; **32**
Bulldogs 61; **61**

Camels 60; **60**
Card games 28; **31**
Carpet toys 66
Carrington Bowles 28
Cars, Toy 66–67; **37, 67**
Carts, Toy 54, 55; **54, 55**
Celluloid dolls 127, 130; **134**
Chad Valley **141**
Character dolls 119, 136–7; **125, 137**
Charlie Chaplin dolls 138
Charlotte, Princess 22
Chemistry sets 31
Chess 69
Chess pieces 69
Chest of drawers, miniature 72; **72**
China, Toy 74; **72, 74, 75**
China-head dolls 127
Chinoiserie style 75
Chippendale 72
Clay doll **4**
Clockwork toys 36, 61; **37, 42**
Clowns 87
Coaches, Toy 16; **16**
Coffers 72–3
Coleman, family 130
Coloured dolls 115, 116, 119, 122, 125, 127; **123, 124**
Commodes, miniature 73
Composition dolls 102, 127
Construction kits 30, 31
Cots, Toy 84–5
Cradles, Toy 7, 62, 84–5; **85**
Crandall's Acrobats 86
Creedmore Bank, The 34; **35**
Cremer 109
Cribs 20
Cuberly, Blondel and Gerbeau 47
Cup-and-ball games 7, 8
Cups, Toy 75

Dark Ages 5
Delany, Mrs Mary 11, 75
Denton Welch Baby House **14**
Devonshire, Duchess of 50
Dinner services 74
Dolls: automated 89; baby 122, 139; 'bonnet' 106; bisque 94, 106, 109, 129, 135, 139; celluloid 127, 130; character 119, 136–7; coloured 115–6,
119, 122, 125, 127, 137; composition 102–3; dolls' house 101, 106; Dutch 99, 127; early 4; fashion 71, 109; French 71, 109–116, 127; German 118–131; india-rubber 113, 134; leather-bodied 109, 120; mass-produced 115, 137; modern 138–9; Oriental 122; papier-mâché 102–3; parian 104–6; pedlar 98, 132–3; porcelain 5, 100–101; Renaissance 7; walking 60, 91, 113, 116; wax 8, 11, 94, 96, 133, 138; wooden 98–9, 132
Dolls' clothes 109, 116, 120
Dolls' Duncan Phyfe 77; **76**
Dolls' house dolls 101, 106
Dolls' house furnishings 14, 80
Dolls' house furniture 13, 14, 15, 76–83; **76, 77**
Dolls' houses 12–15, 74, 78–83; **78, 79, 80, 82, 83**
Donkeys 58
Double-faced doll 118
Draughts 69
Dressel, Cuno & Otto 129; **128, 148**
Droz, Jacquet 89, 90
Drums 7, 8, 17
Dutch dolls 99

Early times 4–5
Edgeworth, Maria 16, 58
Edgeworth, Richard 16
Edison phonograph dolls 124
Educational toys 20, 28–33
Elephants 60; **60**
Ellis wooden doll 99
England 8, 11, 12, 20, 43 52, 54, 55, 61, 74, 97, 132
Ewing, Mrs Juliana Horatia 26

Fakes 85, 109, 111, 133, 153
Farms, Toy 52–3; **52**
Fashion dolls 109; **109**
Fire-places, Toy 77, 79
Flat-backed soldiers 46
Flat irons, Toy 32
Fleischmann 118
'Flirting-eyes' dolls 119; **125**
Footstools, Dolls' **76**
Forts, Toy **45,47**
France 20, 36, 45–7, 50, 68, 86, 97, 102, 105–6, 109–16, 118, 124, 127, 137
Francesco I, of Naples 56

157

Fretwork 77
Friggers 72
Frozen Charlotte **101**
Furniture: Bavarian 76;
dolls' house 13–15,
76–83, **76**, **77**;
miniature 72–3, **72**, **73**

Games 28, 29, 30, 31
Gaultier, Abbé 68
Germany 8, 11, 20, 27, 31,
37, 39–40, 43, 45–8, 50,
52, 75–7, 97, 102, 105–6,
111, 115, 118–31, 137,
140–1
Giles Gingerbread 25
Gin, Emanuele and Emilio 44
Gingerbread soldiers 17
Girls' Own Book (1848) 90
Go-carts 65
Golliwogs 139; **139**
Goody Two-Shoes 25
Gramophones, Toy 88; **89**
Grand Melodrama of the Broken Sword, The 49
Great Exhibition of 1851,
The 32, 111
Greece 68, **4**
Green, J. K. 48
Greenaway, Kate 27
Greiner 103
Grödner Tal 98; **98**
Guns 17
Gutta-percha dolls' heads
134

Hamleys 56, 96
Handwerck, Heinrich 125,
130
Hapsburg, House of 23
Herald Miniatures 47
Heubach 130, 136–7; **136**
Highboys, miniature 73
Hilpert, J. G. 17, 46
History of Little Fanny, The
22; **22**
Holly Trees Museum 58
Hoops 8
Horn books 24, 25; **6**
Hornby 31, 43; **42**
Horses: hobby 4, 6, 18;
pull-along 4, 19, **4**, **57**;
Renaissance 7; rocking
18, 19, 57, **19**, **56**; toy
54–7; velocipede 65,
65; wooden 55
Humpty-Dumpty Circus 87
Huntley and Palmer 37
Hussar 58; **44**

Jack-in-the-boxes 16
Jacob's coronation coach 37

Jameson, J. H. 48, 49
Japan 106
Jenny Lind doll 23
Jigsaw puzzles 16, 20, 29,
30; **28, 29**
Jointed dolls 120, 125,
136–7; **114**, **117**, **121**,
130, 150
Jolly Nigger Boy, The 34
Jumeau 106, 109, 111, 115,
118, 127, 130, 137; **111**
Jumping Jacks 86

Ideal Toy Corporation of
America, The 141
India-rubber dolls and dolls'
heads 113, 134
Italy 44, 55
Ives locomotives 42

Kämmer & Reinhardt 125,
136; **137**
Kestner 137; **66**
Kewpie dolls 139; **144**
Kinetoscope 51
Kitchens, Toy 76; **13, 15**
Kites 17
Kley & Hahn 137
Knucklebones 4
Kubelka factory 130
Kunst und Lehrbüchlein
(1580) 24

Lanternier Company 116; **117**
Leather-bodied dolls 109,
120, 127
Lehmann toys 37
Leipzig Fair of 1903 140
Limbach Porzellanfabrik
130; **130**
Limoges 116
Lines Brothers 57, 66
London Museum, The 38, 40
Louis XIII, Dauphin 7
Lutyens, Sir Edwin 82

McLaughlin Brothers 22
Magic lantern 50; **51**
Magic Ring, The 69
Mail carts 63
Mälzel, Johann Nepomuk 89
Mama-and-Papa doll 113
Mangles, Toy 32
Märklin 42
Mason & Taylor 99
Mayhew, Henry 100
Mechanical toys 34–6, 38–9
Medaille d'Or 1878 111
Meech & Edwards 97
Metal doll Company of
New York 135

Michton, Morris 140
Mickey Mouse 138; **138**
Middle Ages 5, 85
Miniature toys 5, 8, 15,
33, 36, 70, 72, 74; **5**
Model railways 41, 42
Model rooms 8
Models 30, 38–9, 46
Money-boxes 34–5; **34, 35**
Money, Toy 33
Montanari 97; **96**
More, Hannah 25
Morrell, Charles 80, 96
Morrison, Enoch Rise 91
Moving picture-book **26**
Museum of Childhood,
Edinburgh 86
Museum of the City of New
York 79, 133
Musical boxes 88–89; **88**

Naples, Court of 44
Netherlands 8, 12, 14
Newbery, John 25
Noah's Arks 16, 20, 52–3;
53
Norwich House 15, **13**
Nostell Priory 15
Nuremberg 17, 40, 46–7
Nuremberg Baby Houses 8
Nuremberg Kitchens 76; **15**

Oberammergau 52, 98
O'Neill, Rose 139
Optical toys 50–51
Oriental dolls 122, 127–8;
122
Osborne House 32

Panoptique 50
Pantins 8, 86
Paper dolls 22; **22, 23**
Papier-mâché dolls 11,
102–3; **102**, **132**
Parian dolls 104–5, 106;
104, 105
Parisiennes 109, 113
Parlour games **69**
Patterson Brothers 36
Pedlar dolls 98, 132–3;
132, 133
Peep-shows 7, 17
Pellerin brothers 45
Pennyfarthings 65
Penny Toys 38; **38, 39**
Petit, Jacob 101
Picture-blocks 20; **30**
Picture-books 20, 26–7;
24, 25, 26
Picture frames, Toy 77
Pierotti 96, 97; **97**
Piggy Banks 34

158

Pikes, Toy 7
Pilgrim's Progress 25
Pistols, Toy **7**
Plates, Toy 75
Playthings (1897) 52
Pollock, Miss 83
Pollocks 49
Polyphon, Toy 89
Porcelain dolls 5, 100–101; **100**, **101**, **144**
Porzellanfabrik Burggrub 128
Pottery, miniature 74, **5**
Poupards 88
Prams, Dolls' 62; **62**, **63**
Pumpkin heads 94; **94**

Queen Anne dolls 11; **10**
Queen Mary's Dolls' House 80–83; **82**, **83**

Rabery & Delphieu 115, 116
Rag dolls 11
Rattle dolls 11
Rauenstein Porzellanfabrik 130; **66**
Ravca, Bernard 138
Records, Juvenile 88; **89**
Reddington, John 49
Renaissance, The 6; **9**
Rheinische Gummi und Celluloid Fabrik Gesellschaft **134**
Richter and Company 31; **32**
Rohmer 116
Roller skates 16
Roman toys **4**
Roosevelt, Theodore 34, 140
Roullet & Decamps 91, 116, 125
Royal Game of Goose, The 68

Sand pictures 17
Saucers, Toy 75
Schmidt, Bruno 130
Schmitt 116
Schoenau & Hoffmeister 128; **129**
Schoenhut, A. 87; **86**, **128**
School for Young Builders 31
Schreiber, J. F. **48**
Scootles 139
Scrap books 27; **27**
See-saws 66
Set-in glass eyes 104, 135
Sewing-machines, Toy 32; **32**
Sherwood, Mrs Mary Martha 26
Shirley Temple dolls 138
Shops: butcher's 70, **70**; dress 71; grocer's 70–1,
71; milliners' 71; toy 70, 80
Shoulder heads 102, 109, 120, 124, 134; **119**
Sideboards, Toy 73
Sideways-moving mechanisms 119, 125
Simon & Halbig 106, 124–7, 130, 137; **55**, **119**, **124**, **125**, **126**, **129**, **137**
Simonne 109
Simpson, Fawcett and Co. 63
Skelt, Matthew 49
Skittles 4
Sleeping eye mechanisms 93, 94, 119
Slides 50
Slit heads 93, 133; **93**
Smithsonian Institution, Washington 99
Société de Fabrication des Bébés et Jouets 115, 137; **114**, **150**
Sofas 73
Soldiers: army uniforms 45–6; flat-backed 46, **17**; metal 44; model 46, **45**, **46**, **47**; paper 44–5; printed sheets of 45; toy 7, 17, 44–7; wooden 44
Solitaire 69; **69**
Sonneberg 98, 129
Speaking Picture Book, The 26; **25**
Squash heads 94
Staffordshire potteries 35
Stand-up picture books 27
Steiff, Frau Margarete 140
Steiner 137
Stereoscopic card-viewer **51**
Story of a Short Life 26
Strasbourg 45
Stump dolls 8
Sunday toys 20, 53; **21**
Swivel heads 104, 109
Swords 7

Teddy Bears 140–1; **140**, **141**
Teenage-type dolls 127
Theatres, Toy 17, 48; **48**, **49**, **142**
Thaumotropes 50
Think before you act 26
Thorold, Hon Mrs 83
Tin dolls' heads 135; **135**
Tin toys 36–9
Tins 37
Titania's Palace 82
Toulouse-Lautrec, Henri de 138
Tower Toy Guild, The 73
Toys: acrobatic 86–7; boys' 16–17; early 4–5; educational 20; estate-made 55, 66; German 5; mass-produced 20, 36, 82; miniature 5, 8; musical 88–9; pottery 5; Renaissance 6–7, **9**; Sunday 20; tin 36–9
Trade marks 20
Trains: accessories 41; clockwork 43, **42**; electric 43, **41**, **43**; pull-along 40, **40**; scale 41, 43; toy 40–43; wooden 40
Transfers 74, 75
Travellers' samples 72, 74
Treaty of Versailles 47
Tricycles 65
Trimmer, Mrs Sarah 25
Tri-Unial lantern 51
Trumpets 17

Un Petit Ménage 8
Uppark Baby House 15, 80
Upton, Florence 27, 139
Utensils, Toy 76

Velocipedes 65; **64**
Verney, Sir Charles 6
Van Cortlandt Mansion 15
Victoria, Queen 15
Virtue rewarded and Vice Punished 29
Voice mechanisms 94, 115, 127
Votive figures 5

Walking dolls 60, 91, 113, 125
Walking mechanisms 116, 125
Wallis and Son 29
Wax dolls 8, 11, 94, 96, 133; **59**, **93**, **95**, **96**, **97**
Webb **49**
Wedgwood 75
West, William 48; **49**
Wheeled toys 58–67
Wheelbarrows 59
Whistling tongues 119
Wilkinson, Sir Neville 82
Windmills, Toy 6
Wittgenstein family 56
Wooden dolls 5, 8, 11, 98, 99, 132; **98**, **99**, **132**
Wooden tops 98; **99**

Yo-yos 16

Zoëtrope 51, **50**
Zoroaster 49

SOME OTHER TITLES IN THIS SERIES

- Arts
- Domestic Animals and Pets
- Domestic Science
- Gardening
- General Information
- History and Mythology
- Natural History
- Popular Science

Arts
Antique Furniture/Architecture/Clocks and Watches/Glass for Collectors/Jewellery/Musical Instruments/Porcelain/Pottery/Victoriana

Domestic Animals and Pets
Budgerigars/Cats/Dog Care/Dogs/Horses and Ponies/Pet Birds/Pets for Children/Tropical Freshwater Aquaria/Tropical Marine Aquaria

Domestic Science
Flower Arranging

Gardening
Chrysanthemums/Garden Flowers/Garden Shrubs/House Plants/Plants for Small Gardens/Roses

General Information
Aircraft/Arms and Armour/Coins and Medals/Flags/Fortune Telling/Freshwater Fishing/Guns/Military Uniforms/Motor Boats and Boating/National Costumes of the World/Orders and Decorations/Rockets and Missiles/Sailing/Sailing Ships and Sailing Craft/Sea Fishing/Trains/Veteran and Vintage Cars/Warships

History and Mythology
Age of Shakespeare/Archaeology/Discovery of: Africa/The American West/Australia/Japan/North America/South America/Great Land Battles/Great Naval Battles/Myths and Legends of: Africa/Ancient Egypt/Ancient Greece/Ancient Rome/India/The South Seas/Witchcraft and Black Magic

Natural History
The Animal Kingdom/Animals of Australia and New Zealand/Animals of Southern Asia/Bird Behaviour/Birds of Prey/Butterflies/Evolution of Life/Fishes of the world/Fossil Man/A Guide to the Seashore/Life in the Sea/Mammals of the world/Monkeys and Apes/Natural History Collecting/The Plant Kingdom/Prehistoric Animals/Seabirds/Seashells/Snakes of the world/Trees of the world/Tropical Birds/Wild Cats

Popular Science
Astronomy/Atomic Energy/Chemistry/Computers at Work/The Earth/Electricity/Electronics/Exploring the Planets/Heredity The Human Body/Mathematics/Microscopes and Microscopic Life/Physics/Undersea Exploration/The Weather Guide